Writing with Stardust

FOREWORD

'Writing with Stardust' will launch your writing skills into a different orbit. It not only shows you **how to write**, it teaches you **how to look at the world with an 'artist's eye'.**

Spring is described as nature's defibrillator in the book. In the same way, the techniques used here will be the high voltage pacemaker you have been looking for in your writing. You will be swept into a world of enchanting words and magical expressions.

Ready to greet you are females with constellation-blue eyes and megawatt smiles. Males with Hercules-gold hair move like panthers in slow-mo. Thumb plump bumblebees, wings a-thrum, loot from honeypots of mustard-yellow flowers. Sky punching mountains rear into the sky and emblazon their reflections onto moonshine clear lakes. Willowy waterfalls swoop into infinity pools while the stars above sparkle like angel fire. You will smell the candied perfume of the meadow and the woody incense of the forest. Pine and peat, mint and meringue; all the smells and tastes you could wish for are inside. Join me on a multisensory voyage of discovery that will change the way you think forever.

Nature can be a cruel mistress, however. Some chapters are devoted to its dark and stormy side. Blood-red moons leer over boiling seas while mariners try to defy ancient curses. Grim faced men fight for their lives under starless skies and sun blasted deserts burn hotter than Greek fire. You will encounter basilisk-eyed monsters, clouds that wear the garb of the damned and lightning that flashes like the cold, gold prongs of the Apocalypse.

The book provides a platform for students, parents, teachers and lovers of English to launch their descriptive powers into a new orbit. That is why there is a reference to stardust in the title. The grids contain words for five different levels of ability. Whether you are a young English student or a seasoned scribe, you will find that this book will change the way you think about descriptions forever.

There is a Quick Reference Guide at the back of the book. It includes the colours, sounds, smells, sensations and tastes of spring, summer and autumn. There are also 200 magical words that are carefully chosen to transform your essays on nature. One of them is eunoia. This means beautiful thinking. This book promises that if you can combine eunoia with 'Writing with Stardust' you will become a descriptive writer without peer.

*Blog @ www.descriptive writing.wordpress.com

Accompanying video on YouTube entitled Writing with Stardust

Email Liam at oflynn.liam42@gmail.com

TABLE OF CONTENTS

Foreword	1	Table of Contents	2
Different Narrative Styles	3-4	Rivers and Streams	5-10
Using Colour	11	Mountains	12-19
Diction and Imagery	19	The Beach	20-26
Metaphor	27	Waterfalls	28-34
Simile	35	The Forest	36-42
Pathetic Fallacy and Personification	43	Lakes	45-50
Euphony	51	Spring	52-58
Alliteration	59	Summer	60-66
Archaic Words	67	Autumn	68-75
Assonance	76	Winter	77-84
Repetition	85	Monsters	86-92
Triplication	93	The Desert	94-101
Onomatopoeia	102-103	Battle Scenes	104-110
Planning With The Grids Level 1	111-113	The Mist, Rain, Flood Rivers	114-119
Planning with The Grids Level 5	120	Thunder and Lightning	121-129
Using A Dictionary and Psychology	130-131	The Dark Forest	132-139
Spellings	140	Describing Females	141-144
Creativity	145	Describing Females	146-152
Syntax	153	Describing Males	154-157
Using Formulas	158-159	Describing Males	160-166
Describing the Rain	167-177	Describing the Sun	178-179
Describing the Moon	180-183	Describing the Stars	184-185
Describing Spring Grids	186-188	Describing Summer Grids	189-191
Describing Autumn Grids	192-194	Sounds of a Calm Sea	195-196
Sounds of an Angry Sea	197-198	Formulas for a Horizon/Sea Sky	199
100 Magical Words Grid	200	100 Magical Words Grid	201

DIFFERENT NARRATIVE STYLES

There are a range of narrative styles one could use in a descriptive writing passage. By far the most effective is the '**fly-on-the-tree**' technique. This involves the narrator, the person telling the story, pretending that he can see everything from a height, just as the fly can. The narrator should also share the experiences of taste, smell, sound and sensation with the reader, even if the fly can't! It enables the storyteller to give a scope and a sweep to the imagery that might otherwise be too confined and too linear (one dimensional). This technique is also known as **omniscient (all-seeing)** narration. By using this narrative style, one may add variety and give a perspective that is both varied and detailed. It also prevents any monotony setting in for the reader.

The best advice a teacher or parent can give is to tell their budding scribes to look up first, then to look down and, finally, to look around when creating a scene. Try to describe the colour of the sky, the shape of the clouds or the movement of a bird. This creates a setting, just as a landscape painting should have a background. Then add in the smaller details that are under your eye level. Finally, describe the scene as you are walking and let it unfold in front of you.

 Visualise a still painting of a forest in your mind, for example. Let's assume the sky above it has been coloured in with a lush, peacock-blue colour. The clouds are scattered and puffball-white and an eagle is frozen on the canvas with his wings outstretched above you, ready to strike. This is a good start to a passage. It sets the scene by establishing your location (the forest), the season (summer) and the possibility of a dangerous plot developing (i.e. is the eagle hunting you or something else?). Once the background features have been painted in, the plot (story) can begin to take any shape you want it to.

Similarly, if you have that priceless ability to imagine and paint in the smaller details which others might not include, it gives your story creativity and originality. This is what I call '**laser-eyed attention to detail'**. Is it possible you were walking by a river bank in the forest? Could the eagle be an osprey, a fish eagle, perhaps? Can you describe the sound he makes as he swoops past you? Does the silver belly of the fish glisten in his talons in the dawn light? Are the eyes of the eagle nectar-gold and bright or scarecrow-black and lifeless? By including minute details such as these, you are breathing life and imagination into your story. More importantly, these techniques can be developed by any parent or teacher. The key is to have a questing and inquisitive mind when educating a child. Asking them high value questions on colours, images, sounds, smells, sensations and tastes will improve their writing beyond recognition. There is an old adage which states: "In simplicity lies genius". Using the formulas contained in the book will guide students toward the pursuit of excellence.

There is another narrative technique which I call '**zoom narration**'. This can be very effective when you are describing a beach trip, a mountain climbing expedition or a thundery day, amongst others. It requires forward planning, but it is very enjoyable to read when it is completed. In the 'Waterfall' chapter, Level 5, this technique is employed. The idea is to develop your key sounds and images from a faraway perspective. As you get closer, the sounds become louder and the image of the waterfall becomes clearer. The words are sequenced throughout the text, so much so that they seem to appear randomly. The sequence appears in this order:

Sounds- humming/buzzing/whirruping/growling/rumbling

Images- silver tear tracks/threads of watery fabric/loom of liquid silver/sleek robe of a water witch/airy sparkling of its spray

The key to 'zoom narration' is to plan it in advance. Build up a word bank based on the sounds and images needed and then employ them in your passage of writing.

First person narration occurs when a story is written from the point of view of a character in the story. A lot of the time, this would mean that you, as the narrator, intend to tell events in the first person using the personal pronouns **I, my** or **me**. If there are a lot of these pronouns, it is more than likely written in the first person.

Second person narration occurs when a story is directly addressed to the reader. The pronouns used to identify this style are **you** and **your (singular)**. It can be compelling, but it is much rarer as it narrows the range of styles a writer can employ.

Third person narration occurs when the reader watches events unfold as an observer only. The characters in the story have their own world and you are the outsider looking in. The pronouns employed here are **he, she, it, they, them** and **your (plural).** It is probably the most common narrative device.

Alternating-persons narration occurs when the views of several characters are included. It employs a combination of two or more of the above styles. It is common when letters are exchanged between characters or diaries are revealed by the narrator, for example.

An **ants-eye view** is describing a scene from ground level. It is extremely difficult to write a passage of any length while employing this technique. It may be used for something like a summer day on the beach if necessary. It is probably best to avoid it altogether until you have finished reading the tables and formulas contained in the book. Enjoy the read.

RIVERS AND STREAMS

COLOUR

LEVEL 1	LEVEL 2	LEVEL 3	LEVEL 4	LEVEL 5	OTHERS
crystal-blue	sapphire-blue	gemstone-blue	butterfly-blue	dragonfly-blue	
jewel-blue	gem-blue	turquoise-blue	duck egg-blue	kingfisher-blue	

1. The crystal-blue *creek* was very nice.
2. The sapphire-blue *stream* sparkled in the sun.
3. The gemstone-blue *runnel* glittered in the sun.
4. The butterfly-blue *brook* glimmered with its own glory.
5. The kingfisher-blue *rill* was lissome and shimmered like star gleam.

SOUND

splashing	oozing	babbling	murmuring	purring	
trickling	seeping	burbling	thrumming	purling	

1. The river was trickling through the *valley*.
2. The river was oozing through the *meadow*.
3. The river was burbling and bouncing through the *dale*.
4. The gleeful river was thrumming through the *vale*.
5. The cambering river was murmuring and lisping through the mossy *dell*.

SHAPE

twisted	swerved	wound	snaked	meandered	
curved	coiled	weaved	zigzagged	wended	

1. The stream twisted through the *forest*.
2. The stream coiled through the *deciduous forest*.
3. The stream weaved slowly through the *coniferous forest*.

4. The lazy stream zigzagged through the verdant *tropical forest*.

5. The serpentine stream wended its way through the lavender-scented, *alpine forest*.

ACTION

hopped	jumped	sprung	hurdled	bounded	
skipped	leaped	danced	vaulted	jigged	

1. The water skipped over the *rocks*.

2. The water leaped over the *slick rocks*.

3. The spray danced over the *glossy rocks*.

4. The airy spray vaulted over the *moss-slick rocks*.

5. The glitzy spray jigged over the *shocked rocks*.

METAPHORS FOR RIVERS

roads	veins	liquid soul	lifeblood	plasma	
motorways	arteries	pumping heart	liquid spirit	elixir	

1. *Streamlets* are the motorways of the forest.

2. *Brooklets* the veins of the forest.

3. *Burns* are the pumping hearts of the forest.

4. *Becks* provide a liquid spirit to the forest, both refreshing and soothing.

5. *Rivulets* are the plasma of the forest and an elixir for all the flora and fauna.

THE REFLECTION OF WATER USING SIMILES

water flashing	water sparkling	water glowing	water glinting	water glistening	
water flickering	water shimmering	water gleaming	water glittering	water glimmering	

1. The water was flashing *like fairy dust*.

2. The water was shimmering *like sprinkled stardust*.

3. The water was gleaming clearly, *as if fistfuls of diamond dust had been scattered on it*.

4. The water's surface was glittering brightly, *as if millions of sparkling stars* had fallen from the heavens.

5. The water's surface was glimmering with silver, *like billions of scattered sequins glistening together*.

OTHER IMAGES

swans gliding	pebbles tumbling	trout sloshing	twigs twirling	whirlpools whirling	
ducks paddling	butterflies fluttering	dragonflies whizzing	kingfishers fizzing	fisherman's line hissing	

1. Swans were gliding on the water.
2. Pebbles were tumbling through the glassy water.
3. Micro-splashed trout were sloshing and causing ripples on the surface.
4. Kingfishers were fizzing furiously through the crisp air, wings a-blur.
5. A fisherman's line snaked out, hissing and fizzing, whipping into the icy-fingered mist.

SENSATION

refreshing	stimulating	thirst-quenching	
energizing	invigorating	thirst-slaking	

1. I took a drink from the fresh stream. It was energizing.
2. My thirst was overwhelming. I drank deep and it was invigorating.
3. I quaffed deep from the gurgling river. It was thirst-slaking.

SMELL

scent	fragrance	perfume	
aroma	waft	cologne	

1. The scent from the old forest was very sweet.
2. The fragrance of the grizzled forest was heady and warm.
3. The swirling perfume of the time-worn forest was intoxicating.

TASTE

yummy	lush	scrumptious	
rich	delicious	sublime	

1. The riverbank grew wild edibles. I picked a few and they were yummy.
2. The crinkly quilt of the floor was studded with wild basil. I tasted one and it was delicious.
3. The crackly mattress of the forest was strewn with wild wood sorrel. I bit into one and it was sublime.

LEVEL 1: BASIC SENTENCES

1. I saw a **jewel-blue stream** in the forest. **COLOUR**
2. It was **splashing** as it moved through the trees. **SOUND**
3. It **curved** gently through the forest. **SHAPE**
4. It **hopped** over the rocks happily. **ACTION**
5. My friend told me that **rivers are the roads of the forest**. **METAPHOR**
6. This one was **flickering like glitter** on the surface. **SIMILE**
7. I could see **a family of ducks** paddling on the water. **OTHER IMAGES**
8. I took a drink. It was very **refreshing**. **SENSATION**
9. The **aroma** of the forest was great. **SMELL**
10. It drew me to a berry bush. I ate one and it **tasted rich**. **TASTE**

LEVEL 2: A BASIC PARAGRAPH

I spied a **gem-blue** stream in the forest. It was **seeping** and dribbling as it **swerved** through the trees. It **jumped** for joy over the timeworn rocks. I heard once that **rivers are the arteries of the forest**. This one was **sparkling like tinsel**. The **fluttering butterflies** drifted over it lazily. I bent my head down to drink from it. It was very **stimulating**. The **aroma** of the forest was very powerful. I plucked a few berries and they were **lush and fruity** to the tongue.

LEVEL 3: CREATIVE PARAGRAPHS

A **turquoise-blue** stream **wound** its merry way through the forest. **Babbling and burbling**, it **sprung** over the limestone rocks in its way. Pebbles whisked about in the under wash like pieces of glitter. **Streams are the liquid soul of the forest**, and this one was glowing. **Chords of soft light** speared down from above, bathing its surface in gold. It was glinting with little sparkles, **like a thousand diamonds blessed with an inner fire**. A galaxy of **dragonflies fizzed** through the beams of light, wings a-glitter in the sun. The hedgerows were pregnant with berries and we tasted some. They **energized us** with their **pleasant waft**. The **delicious taste** stayed with us all the way home.

LEVEL 4: ADVANCED PARAGRAPHS

I was the first to chance upon the brook. It was a fragile, **duck-egg blue** colour, like the subtle sweep of a painter's brush. **Seeping and snaking** smoothly past all obstacles, it managed to **hurdle** the river's boulders also. **Twigs twirled** on its **murmuring** surface, little messengers from the mountain trees where they had come from. The brook flowed over the pebbled riverbed. It sounded like the airy, velvety whirl of a starling flock.

The mountains stood silently in the background, a brooding presence of sky punching majesty. Brooches of snow covered their lofty peaks, encircling them in wreaths of angel-white. A weeping waterfall poured from a gash in the rock face. It looked like a slide of silk-blue flowing down the mountain. Carrying its load of ice crystals, it appeared hemmed with silver. A distant thrumming sound emanated from it, like the steady rumble of a drum roll. **Glinting brightly**, it fed the river, **the lifeblood of the forest**. It was an awe-inspiring sight. My gaze returned to the swirling brook. I could see now how the water had gained its glassy clarity. The run off from the ice made it appear varnish clear and the surface glinted as if dream dust had been scattered over it. Speckled trout drifted under the shady eaves of the bank, flicking their tails lazily. If a juicy fly happened to pass them, they would explode from the pebbled bed like angels of death. Arcing into the air, their bodies glistening, they hovered briefly, performing the ballet of the river. Then, with a plunking sound, they would dart back to the shadowed depths, their catch already safe in their spotted bellies. The watery grace of the river seemed magical to me at that moment.

The riverbank was lined with pods of wild peas. The pods were black, but inside there were tiny, succulent, fresh peas. I tasted one and it was **scrumptious**. Never did food wrapped in the devil's cloak taste so good! Bending down, I scooped a hand through the water and drank my fill. It was **thirst-quenching.** I leaned my back against a rock and closed my eyes, enjoying the sun's warmth. The **sweet perfume** of the forest drifted to my nostrils as I reflected on the beauty of nature.

LEVEL 5: COMPLEX WRITING: THE FISHERMAN

We arrived just before dawn. The quiet of the world was wondrous to behold. It was as still as a crypt and even the moth flutter had died down.

The mist gave us a hint that we were still in the nether world between night and day. It lingered over the river like a phantom's veil. Soundless, voiceless and soulless, it slowly slid away. Its misty fingers clasped despairingly at the body of water below it one last time. Then it faded, allowing the Technicolor of nature to be turned up like a light switch.

The river that **meandered** through the forest was a bright, **dragonfly-blue.** A soft, watery murmur of elegance came from its sensuous journey over the chalky bed. **Purring and purling**, it flowed with all the smooth grace of rippling satin. In places, its languorous passage was blocked by obdurate rocks. Heedless, it **bounded** over their stony armour, carelessly tossing bubbles of spray into the air. The **spray was glimmering like tiny crystals**. It was an **elixir for the soul** to witness nature's sights and sounds in the glory of the morning.

Further up the river, **a lone fisherman** stood framed by the hunched mountains in the background. The gentle whirring of his reel came to our ears. It clicked now and then, followed by the swish of his line as it creased the air. Face tight with concentration, he flicked his wrist and the fly zipped over to rest on a whirlpool. Bobbing with the current, it suddenly disappeared. The tip of his rod bent, jerked, vibrated and plunged violently downwards.

A leviathan of the deep rose up from the gritty depths of the river. He burst through the surface with a frenzied leap, vaulting into the cold air. At the same time, the line made a snappy, hissing sound. The fisherman staggered back a step. He looked forlorn as the fish of his lifetime slapped the water on his way back to freedom. Then came the thousand yard stare common to all the vanquished fishers of the river. He stood motionless, his gaze eventually toing and froing from rod to river and back again. We felt sorry for him and moved away silently, leaving him wrapped in his own dejection.

We stopped by a glopping spring to get a drink of water. It was arctic pure and **thirst-slaking**. The forests **earthy cologne** swirled around us and we gathered some wild hazelnuts. They were as **sublime** as the river that nourished the forest.

mutton	lamb	beef	
pot roast	bubbling broth	sizzling steak	

1. The scent of stewed mutton came drifting up to us.
2. The welcoming aroma of a bubbling broth came to our noses.
3. We smelled a sizzling steak being fried far below us and it was sublime.

TASTE

astral	cosmic	astronomical	
stellar	galactic	otherworldly	

1. The pot roast was stellar.
2. The chargrilled lamb was cosmic with the beans.
3. We guzzled the flame-fried beef and it was otherworldly.

LEVEL 1: BASIC SENTENCES

1. The mountains were **bone-white**. **COLOUR**
2. A wall of snow came **crashing** down. **SOUND**
3. The mountains were **crinkled** at the top. **SHAPE**
4. They were **sky-piercing**. **ACTION**
5. The **foot** of one mountain was covered in mist. **PATHETIC FALLACY**
6. The mountain peaks were **like a row of arrow tips**. **SIMILE**
7. We could see some **deer** clattering across a mountain. **OTHER IMAGES**
8. The air felt **ice cold**. **SENSATION**
9. We could smell **stewed mutton** coming from a camp. **SMELL**
10. We tasted some and it was **astral**. **TASTE**

LEVEL 2: A BASIC PARAGRAPH

The mountains were **vampire-white**. A wave of white snow went **rumbling** down the sides. They were all **crumpled** at the base. They were **sky-stabbing** at the top. The **legs** of the mountains were very wide. The peaks of the mountains were **like harpoon tips**. They were shrouded in **ghost-grey mist**. The air was **chilling and numbing**. We could smell a **pot roast** being cooked. We tasted some and it was **stellar**.

LEVEL 3: CREATIVE PARAGRAPHS

The serrated mountains loomed in the distance. We made our way towards them as we had to make base camp by nightfall. They were **flour-white** and brooded over the land. Just as we approached, a chute of snow detached itself and went **trundling** down one of the mountains. It slid over the **knotted** edge and then went crashing into the chasm below. The silence that followed was spine chilling. It froze our marrow to think that we would be climbing in those conditions tomorrow.

 The **heaven-touching** apex of the mountain was drenched in brilliant light. Spikes of thin light impaled the snow in a bristling, moving line. We assumed that the heat had displaced the snow from **the hip** of the time chiselled mountain. All across our line of sight, the tips of the mountain range stuck up **like a row of thorns.** Swaddled around them were **necklaces of powdery snow**. The air became **arctic cold** as we came closer to base camp. The unmistakable whiff of **chargrilled lamb** wafted to our noses. Dinner that night was **cosmic**.

LEVEL 4: ADVANCED PARAGRAPHS

We looked up fearfully at the **angel-white** mountains. They looked ominous. As we watched in horror, a **grumbling** sound came from the largest of them.

A mighty chunk of snow came toppling down from the **gnarled** face of the mountain. It looked like a cascade of white as it tumbled and rumbled downwards. With a deafening roar, it plummeted over the **hoary shoulder** and settled in a mighty heap. Then there was a dreadful silence. Nothing stirred. Nothing sounded. Nothing sang.

The silence was ruptured by the slow, mournful howl of one of our camp dogs. He could sense that climbing those zephyr haunted mountains tomorrow would invite disaster. Yet climb them we would, as that was our goal. Our sponsor would pay dearly for evidence of the yeti and we were determined to provide it. We were at five thousand feet and the air was thin and crisp. The **snow-cloaked** mountains hemmed us in on all sides, daring us to reach their **stalagmite shaped** peaks.

A vast sheet of ice lay in front of us. We had reached a wide plateau. It was eerie and looked Cossack-cold. It was a featureless terrain, a place with a harsh and stark beauty. It reminded me of the opening scene of 'Frankenstein', when he clumped through the zombie-white snow. Stunted dwarf trees had been seen lower down, but not even they could survive this.

Devoid of life and leaf, the rocky acoustics made it sound like a crypt. The only sounds were the huffing of dogs, the swish of skis and the curses of men.

The dimming sun framed a great sweep of **lonely, birdshell-blue sky**. It was our cue to set up camp before attacking the summit tomorrow. Night's dark mantle closed in around us and the thermometer plunged. It became **Siberian cold** so we set up a fire. Supper that night was **a bubbling broth** and it tasted **galactic**. We all stared into the crackling fire, each of us wrapped in our own thoughts. Tomorrow would bring the risk of death and disaster with it.

LEVEL 5: COMPLEX WRITING: THE LONELY TOMB

They hated us. Their complexion may have been **halo-white**, but they hated us all the more for it. We were standing in a vast pan of emptiness, with only sky above and death below. It was a great gash of valley half way up the Himalayas, stretching out for endless miles. On either side, indomitable mountains loomed, enfolding in on our minds with their might. We knew they hated us as much as the last expedition, whose remains we were sent to find.

The winds glacial breath swept through the valley, licking it with its icy caress. It neither moaned nor sighed, nor made any sound at all. It simply haunted the valley, constantly gnawing at us with its ravening fangs. A **thundering** sound suddenly filled the air, replacing the silence. A huge swathe of snow detached itself from the **rumpled** side of the mountain. It tobogganed past the **furrowed brow**, swooping towards its own ruin. Then, with a mighty crash and the phuffing sound of a blanket billowing, it finally came to rest.

A deathlike shush spilled into the valley. All was silent. All was still. We peered up at the **snow-wreathed** summit to see if there would be another avalanche. Above it, the sky leered down at us with a manacle-grey hue, like an ashen face. It seemed to compress down upon our minds, such was its throttling effect. Our hearts became heavy as both sky and mountain entombed us with an alien emptiness. The mountains seemed to us to be as inflexible and dangerous **as a dragon's back**. Bereft of either sound or spirit, we stood there transfixed. Even the silence seemed strangled at that moment. We felt like pasty shadows, insignificant, under the immensity of the cadaverous sky. The lonely cry of an eagle suddenly rang out, giving us hope. Not all life had been garrotted out of this godforsaken land.

We walked on, marvelling as the sun broke through the bank of iron-grey cloud. It reflected back to us in a trident of blazing-blues, star flame-silvers and wizard-whites. Our boots crunched through the powdered snow. They detonated like muffled grenades every time we stepped, banishing the eerie stillness to oblivion. The **algid**, rarefied air made breathing difficult, but we soldiered on. A bizarre, yowling sound would occasionally erupt from above us. Whether it was the dreaded **abominable snowman** or the wind rushing through a discarded rucksack, we would never know.

Dinner that night was sombre, each of us locked in the prison of our own fears. The **sizzling steak** we partook of was **astronomical**. Yet if truth be told, it felt like The Last Supper. Doom-mongering would serve no purpose, so we retired to our tents silently, with leaden hearts and flagging spirits. Tomorrow would bring perdition with it. There were bodies to be retrieved and perhaps new ones to grace the mountains.

DICTION AND IMAGERY

We are all shackled by the limits of our imagination, and therefore, by definition, our language. This is a phrase I use constantly in the classroom. In simpler terms, when it comes to writing, we are what we think. In order for students to express themselves fully, they need a store of words to draw from. That is why the book has so many word banks which share a theme. When a student needs to access a word from one of the banks, it makes it easier that they are structured and compartmentalised in their minds. Even if it is a mixed ability class, there will always be a simple word to draw from or a new word to challenge them.

That is why **diction**, their **choice of words**, is so important. English as a language is as fluid, ever-changing and adaptable as a child's mind is. It is constantly being challenged by new words and phrases, just as an English student should be. Examples of modern words seeping into the lexicon are: **squillions, kidult and glamazonian**. They are included in the book as there is no reason not to. They all add to the richness of the fabric of English, although they may not be in the dictionary. If they can convey a character trait or idea that another word can't, they have every right to be included in the language. In this book, there are two words that I had to invent in order to recreate the sound of a waterfall and the fast, silvery ripple of a dragonfly's wings. That's because I didn't feel the words available in the dictionary did them justice. I chose **whirruping** for the former and **a-glirr** for the latter. In the context of a child's writing, the ethos is the same. Reward creativity and a child who uses imaginative metaphors and unique diction, even if it doesn't fit a conventional style.

Using **imagery** in a passage of writing follows the same guidelines. An image is the building block of English. Without imagery, there can't be any connection between a writer and a reader. Teaching a child how to use imagery has to be nurtured. This is where the analogy of a painting comes in. Ask them to visualise a forest, as was done in the 'Narrative Style' section. This time ask them to fill in the details *below* the trees. The weaker children will struggle, perhaps concentrating on people, animals and flowers. Those who are more advanced will include a wider variety of images. It could be a river with a kingfisher flying over it or more exotic images such as a unicorn. That is because they can create better images in their **'mind's eye'**, their imagination. Sometimes it is a natural ability, but it is usually because of background factors such as access to books, parental encouragement or an inspiring teacher. The same rule applies as it did to the use of diction. Children need a base, a bank of information, to draw from. Otherwise, they will forever be shackled by the limits of their imagination.

THE BEACH

COLOUR

LEVEL 1	LEVEL 2	LEVEL 3	LEVEL 4	LEVEL 5	OTHERS
butter-gold beach	moon glint-gold beach	sunrise-gold beach	lightning-gold beach	earthlight-gold beach	
flax-gold beach	moon glow-gold beach	sunset-gold beach	mother lode-gold beach	earthshine-gold beach	

1. The **sand** shone like butter-gold.
2. The **seashore** was moon glint-gold.
3. The **shoreline** lit up with a sunset-gold glow.
4. The **coastline** was bathed in a mother lode-gold aura.
5. The **strand** was immersed in an earthshine-gold corona.

SOUND

LEVEL 1	LEVEL 2	LEVEL 3	LEVEL 4	LEVEL 5	OTHERS
sleepy sea	dozy sea	slothful sea	slumbering sea	reposing sea	
snoozy sea	dreamy sea	sluggish sea	supine sea	languorous sea	

1. **Stems** of light drizzled the sleepy sea.
2. **Sinews** of light showered the dreamy sea.
3. **Rods** of golden light rebounded off the sluggish sea.
4. **Tendrils** of slanted light arrowed onto the supine sea.
5. **Wands** of magical light caressed the languorous sea.

SHAPE

LEVEL 1	LEVEL 2	LEVEL 3	LEVEL 4	LEVEL 5	OTHERS
an arc of beach	a hook of beach	a sickle of beach	a dome of beach	a crook of beach	
a bow of	a horseshoe	a scythe of	a half- moon	a crescent of	

beach	of beach	beach	of beach	beach	

1. An arc of beach lay under a *vast sky*.
2. A hook of beach sat under an *infinite sky*.
3. The beach was shaped like a sickle under the *endless sky*.
4. The *limitless sky* gazed down upon the dome of beach.
5. The *boundless sky* surveyed the crescent of golden beach.

METAPHORS WITH THICK LIGHT

lanterns of light	towers of light	waves of light	streams of light	pillars of light	
cylinders of light	sheets of light	rivers of light	streamers of light	columns of light	

1. Lanterns of light *flooded* the sea with their glow.
2. Sheets of light *drowned* the sea with their brilliance.
3. Waves of light *submerged* the beach in a golden glow.
4. The sea was *saturated* by streams of heaven-leaking light.
5. The rippling sea was *immersed* by columns of heaven-spilling light.

TANS

nut-brown	conker-brown	sun-blasted	Day-Glo	perma-tan	
leather-brown	coconut-brown	sun-stained	after-glow	uber-tan	

1. People *strolled by* with nut-brown tans.
2. Tourists *ambled past* with conker-brown faces.
3. Beachgoers *lazed along* with sun-stained bodies.
4. Sun worshippers nonchalantly *idled by* with after-glows.
5. Sun seekers *meandered lazily past* me with their perma-tans.

KNITTING TERMS FOR A SEA SKY

edged	knitted	sewn	laced	seamed
threaded	stitched	fringed	hemmed	embroidered

1. The **blanket** of sky was edged with silver.
2. The **cloak** of paradise-blue sky was knitted with clouds.
3. The unending **veil** of sea sky was fringed with tuft-clouds.
4. The measureless **drape** of polestar-blue was laced with puffball-white.
5. The unfathomable **mantle** of lodestar-blue sky was embroidered with silver at the horizon.

OTHER IMAGES

kites flapping	donkeys braying	seagulls squawking	boats bobbing	sea rippling
children squealing	horses whinnying	seagulls squabbling	yachts lolling	waves creasing

1. Kites were flapping next to the **peaceful** sea.
2. Horses were whinnying next to the **placid** sea.
3. The seagulls were squabbling together over the **tranquil** sea.
4. Sleek yachts were lolling and dipping in the **docile** sea.
5. The waves were creasing and causing swirls in the **serene** sea.

SENSATION

sun baked	heat grilled	glare charred
sun toasted	heat roasted	glare scorched

1. The midday sun baked our bodies.
2. The afternoon sun grilled us slowly.
3. The sun's glare charred our bodies to a crispy gold.

SMELL

salty	oily	brackish	
chlorine	tangy	saline	

1. The air smelled salty.

2. The sea air smelled oily.

3. The saline air had a brackish tang to it.

TASTE

spicy sauces	barbecued chicken	briny lobster	
coal-fired peppers	sulfurous mustard	fried onions	

1. The coal-fired peppers were delicious.

2. They went well with the barbecued chicken.

3. The fried onions were a gastronomic delight.

LEVEL 1: BASIC SENTENCES

1. The beach was **flax-gold**. **COLOUR**

2. We heard the **snoozy** sea lap gently. **SOUND**

3. We walked on **a bow of beach**. **SHAPE**

4. **Cylinders of light** moved across the sea. **METAPHORS**

5. The other tourists were **leather-brown**. **TANS**

6. The neon-blue sky was **threaded** with silver. **KNITTING TERMS FOR THE SKY**

7. **Children were squealing** on the beach. **OTHER IMAGES**

8. The **sun toasted** our skin. **SENSATION**

9. The sea air smelled of **chlorine**. **SMELL**

10. The **spicy sauces** in the burger burned our tongues. **TASTE**

LEVEL 2: A BASIC PARAGRAPH

The beach we walked on was **moon glow-gold**. The sea looked **dozy** as it rested in the afternoon glow. We were walking on **a horseshoe of beach**. **Towers of radiant light** soaked the sea with their beauty. The holiday makers we saw all had **coconut-brown faces**. Clown-hatted donkeys were **braying** loudly as children pulled their tails. The burning **sun roasted** us like nuts in an oven. The sea sky seemed **threaded** with silver. A warm, **tangy odour** came from the sea as we walked towards a hot dog stand. The **sulfurous mustard** burned us nearly as much as the sun.

LEVEL 3: CREATIVE PARAGRAPHS

It's not often you get to see a **sunrise-gold** beach. That was our privilege as we gazed out at the **slothful sea**. Ebbing ever so gently, it looked at peace in its jade-green gown. It felt like we were walking on a carpet of candy floss, such was its softness. The golden sand swept around in **a scythe of beach**, hemmed in by towering dunes. Far out to sea, **rivers of pulsing light** saturated the sea with gold. Only the occasional tourist walked past us. There was an absence of **sun-blasted bodies** in this Babylon of beaches.

The horizon seemed to be **stitched** with a silver line. The **seagulls were squawking** over our heads and squabbling for morsels from the hotel kitchen. As the **sun scorched** our bodies to a crisp, a funfair of barbecued aromas drifted towards us. The **saline tang** of the sea mingled with the cuisine, adding salt to its appeal. We decided to obey our rumbling stomachs and eat. Lobster on a bed of watercress was our fare that afternoon. It tasted tender and **briny** and the shell food sauce had a hint of bouquet to it.

LEVEL 4: ADVANCED PARAGRAPHS

We stood on the cliff. By chance, we had found the Mecca of coves. We could see a fracture of white sand, a gash of zephyr-haunted cliffs and a wide slash of bay. It was a watery wonderland and the beach was drenched in a **lightning-gold**, dawn haze. The mighty heap of sea flowed in its astral-blue smoothness from the horizon in. The horizon itself was a thin seam where the canopy of sky and the plane of sea **hemmed** each other into a line of silver. It was as if they had been welded into an extended splinter of perfection. In the distance, **streamers of tapered light** splayed out, flowing through cracks in the cloud. We decided to clamber down to the beach.

Slumbering in its blue robe, the sea greeted us and the **half-moon of beach** softly. The sand was floury underfoot and a feathery, sugar-white of hue. A single yacht **bobbed and lolled** in the incoming tide, like a toy in a bath. Its lights winked saucily as the wave-crests rose gently. Looking around the secluded beach, we didn't see any of the normal sights; tourists with **Day-Glo tans**, tacky stands or chattering hawkers. We realised that we were standing in the gateway of paradise. The siren call of the sea was soothing, the wave music welcome. It was like being wrapped in comforting cellophanes of warm sounds and soft light.

Our serenity was ruptured by the raucous cry of a gull. The rocky hollowness of the cliffs made it seem mournful and cavern loud. It echoed at first with a mournful sound, recoiling from the cliff-rock. It rebounded and its vibration was resonating in the spacious air. The bouncing and distortion of sound rang it out once more. Then it foundered and finally faded away into nothingness.

Our serenity had been interrupted. We decided to make our way home. The rising **sun laminated us** with its warmth and **a theatre of pelagic smells** wafted from the steaming seaweed. **It took the edge off our hunger** and we decided not to eat.

Our footprints in the sand followed us all the way home. Heavens hideaway had been a transcendental experience and we resolved to do it again someday.

LEVEL 5: USING 10 COLOURS TOGETHER

I sauntered along the shimmering sand. It was **unicorn-white** and as soft as sugar. It felt like powdered chalk dust under my feet. In places, it was speckled with glistening, wave tossed shells. The beach was torc shaped and fringed by **jasper-green** palm trees.

Out in the bay, a venerable lighthouse seemed bolted to a clump of naked rock. It jutted up like a round tower from the confined deep of the ocean. Coiling hoops of **vault-black** were wrapped around it, split by **bleach-white** veins.

Closer to the shore, the naked rocks were limpet-kilted. The waves were slushing off them, their **crystal-silver** crests sparkling like pulverized diamonds. The sea was gin clear beyond the tide line, looking paralyzed under a **luminol-blue** sky.

Perma-tanned tourists passed by, burnished to a **walnut-brown** by the sun. Most of them moved with the languid and louche air of the 'nouveau riche', like panthers in slow-mo. They were here to chillax in this **rapture-blue** gateway of paradise.

It was a Noah's-ark-safe utopia. The beach shone like **earthlight-gold** as I ambled along and I embraced the warmth of the sun. As it went down, striations of **cerise-pink** crept into the sky. I knew now why this beach was called the jewel of the Mediterranean.

LEVEL 5: USING 30 SOUNDS TOGETHER

I **ambled** along the melodious seashore. Where the breakers **crashed**, the pebbled sand was alive with sound. The ebbing sea **scraped** the grit **slushily**, **slurpily hissed** at them, **polished**, **washed** and released them.

They **fizzed** and **swished**, **sluiced** and **sizzled**, before finally settling, **raspy** and **seething**.

The **flux** and **reflux** of the tide sounded like a lake of **sloppy** mercury. Sibilantly **hissing**, the wave song was magnified by the wide **sweep** of sea and sky.

It made it appear as if I was walking in surround sound and embalmed with nature's music.

The **symphonious** mermaids call of the sea was uplifting, like a potion for the soul. The **echo** of a thousand tides **washed** over me and I **quaffed** deep from its heady magic.

Someone had **sprinkled** dream dust on this slice of heaven millennia ago and the memory of it still **swirled** around. The Mediterranean **pulse** of the sea became **muted** and **metronomic**.

A delicious smell **wafted** in the air and I decided to **laze** my way towards it.

LEVEL 5: USING SMELLS/ SENSATIONS/ TASTES

A carnival of scents floated in the air. My stomach rumbled and growled. It was an intoxicating mix, containing a whisper of coconut and a suspicion of citrus. It smelled sumptuous. My eyes watered and my palate tingled with the sudden hunger.

There was another, more powerful scent in this symphony of aromas and it began to dominate. It was the unmistakable smell of charcoal sear. I licked my lips and smacked my chops in anticipation. Flame-grilled meat was on the menu and I could almost taste the splattering juices dripping from the tender centre. I could pick out the tangy, divine rumour of spitted calf gliding towards me also.

The thought of the steak fat dribbling and splashing onto the hot griddle tantalized me. The scorching and sizzling of the meat made my legs wobble. A rumour of barbecue sauce, spicy and hot, joined the broth of lavish smells. It was a sensory overload.

I decided to run towards the chef before it was all gone. When I eventually bit into the succulent steak, the squirting blood was lava hot. It tasted exquisite. The fried onions with mushrooms were mouth-watering and the steak was out of this world. My endorphins went into orbit. It was the most blissful and savoury meal that I have ever tasted.

METAPHOR

A **metaphor is a comparison of two things without using as or like**. It is also known as **parabole**. Metaphors can infuse a sparkling vitality to anyone's writing if used in the right manner. In many ways, they are a portal to a higher plane of thinking. The best example I can give for this is the word 'mountain'. It is quite extraordinary that there is no other word for 'mountain' in the English language. You may argue that words like alp, hillock, peak and mount are similar and you would be right. They are similar, but they are not the same. How do you then write an essay or passage on a mountain without constantly referring to the same name over and over? Surely this makes it very monotonous for the reader? The answer is to use metaphors to help the reader visualise what you are trying to convey. Using metaphors for shapes such as mountains enables you to use the **'artist's eye'**. This is where the higher plane of thinking comes in. If you draw the shape of a mountain range and ask a student to describe what they see, they will probably say a mountain range. If you encourage them to give other examples of that shape, it is very gratifying to hear the answers. The key word here is to encourage them. It is a technique that has to be nurtured, not acquired. What you are essentially asking them to do is to give a list of **metaphors for the mountain**. They will move through the gears pretty quickly, from **shark's fins** to **rose thorns** to **talon tips**. Then you can encourage the sentences to look like this:

"The peaks had **the shape of a row of shark's fins**".

Now they will link the outline of an object to another shape regularly when asked, forming metaphors quite easily. The **'artist's eye'** should be encouraged for trees, waterfalls, beaches, clouds and any other parts of nature that have a contour, a shape or an outline. A tree thus becomes **the skyscraper of the forest**, a waterfall becomes **a silver slide** and **feathery clouds** hang over **sickle-shaped beaches**.

Over time, the metaphors can become more advanced and creative. Lips are **sugar sweet**, deserts are **Satan's sauna** and **veins of lightning** pierce through **ribbons of mist**. There are no limits to how original a child can be with metaphors. The secret is to let them visualise how one object or idea can be associated with another. The end result shall be a passage of writing that is unique, vibrant and thrumming with the energy of metaphors.

WATERFALLS

COLOUR

LEVEL 1	LEVEL 2	LEVEL 3	LEVEL 4	LEVEL 5	OTHERS
arctic-blue	Atlantic-blue	Pacific-blue	Caribbean-blue	lagoon-blue	
aquarium-blue	Atlantis-blue	Mediterranean-blue	Neptune-blue	riparian-blue	

1. The arctic-blue waterfall was *streaked* with silver.
2. The Atlantic-blue waterfall was *veined* with silver edge.
3. The Pacific-blue waterfall was *grooved* with a silver lining.
4. The Neptune-blue cataract was *inlayed* with streaks of silver.
5. The lagoon-blue cascade was *striated* with glints of silver.

THE SOUND OF A GENTLE WATERFALL

dripping	gushing	spraying	showering	sprinkling	
drizzling	gurgling	swishing	spurting	spluttering	

1. The dripping of the waterfall made a *ringing* sound.
2. The gurgling of the water caused a tinny *ping* like a bell.
3. The spraying of the water caused a magical *plinking* sound.
4. The baptismal *chinking* of showering water on rock was musical.
5. The chrismal *tinkle* of the sprinkling waterfall was wondrous to behold.

THE SOUND OF A ROARING WATERFALL

rushing	surging	smashing	clamorous	whooshing	
pounding	boiling	thundering	clangourous	cacophonous	

1. The waterfall was rushing down in *anger*.
2. The waterfall was boiling over the rocks with *rage*.

3. The waterfall was smashing into the rocks in *frenzy*.
4. The clangourous waterfall was spitting with its *hissy fits*.
5. The cacophonous waterfall was buffeting the rocks in a *zealous rage*.

ACTION

flowed	swooped	crashed	surged	spiralled	
tumbled	plunged	toppled	plummeted	cascaded	

1. The waterfall flowed like a silver *ramp*.
2. The waterfall swooped down like a liquid *slide*.
3. The waterfall crashed down like a silky *chute* of silver.
4. The waterfall surged down like a velvety *weir* of silver.
5. The graceful waterfall cascaded down like nature's *liquid loom*.

A DIVINITY-POOL

infinity-pool	serenity-pool	ecstasy-pool	rapture-pool	eternity-pool	
bliss-pool	mystique-pool	enchantment-pool	rhapsody-pool	tranquillity-pool	

1. The infinity-pool was very *clear*.
2. The mystique-pool was *see-through* to the bottom.
3. The enchantment-pool was as *transparent* as glass.
4. The rapture-pool was as *limpid* and clear as a diamond.
5. The eternity-pool was as *pellucid* as a window on a summer's day.

THE TEXTURE OF A WATERFALL

silk	suede	velvet	honey	dew	
satin	syrup	velour	aluminium	mercury	

1. The silky waterfall was *dinging* with joy.
2. The suede soft waterfall was *pealing* with pleasure.
3. The velvet-silver waterfall was *jingling* off the rocks.

4. The waterfall flowed like honey, **chiming** gently off the rocks.

5. The waterfall poured as smoothly as mercury, **clinking** and lilting like little bells.

OTHER IMAGES

grasses swaying	frogs croaking	geese grazing	willows wilting	cascades sissing
flowers nodding	fish darting	herons spearing	wagtails bobbing	cataracts susurrating

1. Grasses were swaying next to the **slick** waterfall.

2. Fish were darting under the **sleek** waterfall.

3. Stilt-legged herons were spearing fish next to the **slinky** waterfall.

4. A grove of sad willows brooded next to the **sensuous** waterfall.

5. The cascade was sissing as it flowed **sylph-like** over the gravelly bed.

SENSATION

shaking	trembling	quivering
shivering	shuddering	quaking

1. We stood under the waterfall and we began shivering.

2. Its icy tongue of water had us trembling beneath it.

3. It was tundra cold and our quaking bodies couldn't take it anymore.

SMELL

honey sweet	nougat sweet	glucose sweet
treacle sweet	syrup sweet	nectar sweet

1. The aroma of the flowers was treacle sweet.

2. The scent of the bluebells was syrup sweet.

3. The sweet fragrance of the daffodils was glucose sweet.

TASTE

| heavenly | angelic | unearthly | |
| divine | Godly | ambrosial | |

1. We had a riverside picnic. The homemade jam was heavenly.
2. The fresh fruit was angelic under the gas flame-blue sky
3. The grilled brook trout was ambrosial and titillated our taste buds.

LEVEL 1: BASIC SENTENCES

1. The waterfall was **aquarium-blue**. **COLOUR**
2. It was **drizzling** onto the rocks. **SOFT SOUNDS**
3. The larger waterfall was **pounding** the rocks. **LOUD SOUNDS**
4. It **tumbled** down the mountain. **ACTION**
5. The **bliss-pool** at the bottom was varnish clear. **A DIVINITY-POOL**
6. It looked like a wall of blue **satin** threaded with silver. **TEXTURE**
7. The **flowers** next to it were nodding gently. **OTHER IMAGES**
8. It was **freezing** and we were shaking with the cold. **SENSATION**
9. The flowers growing nearby had a **honey sweet smell**. **SMELL**
10. We ate an ice cream cone on the bank and it was **divine**. **TASTE**

LEVEL 2: A BASIC PARAGRAPH

The waterfall was **Atlantis-blue**. It was **gushing** over the rocks. At its widest point, it was **surging** and **plunging** down the mountain. It had a beautiful **serenity-pool** at the bottom. It was veneer clear. The waterfall flowed as smoothly as **syrup**. The **frogs croaking** nearby added to the wonderful sounds. We threw ourselves under the waterfall. It was so cold that we started **shuddering**. We collapsed on the bank and let the **nougat sweet smell** of flowers wash over us. Later we had some ham sandwiches and they were **Godly**.

LEVEL 3: CREATIVE PARAGRAPHS

The waterfall was **Mediterranean-blue** and magical. It was **swishing** over the rocks joyfully. It was **thundering** down into the pool like a gigantic water spout. When it **toppled** into the

ecstasy-pool, it foamed it at the bottom. The rest of the pool was as clear as cellophane, enabling us to see down into the rocky bottom. Fronds of forest-green plants waved gently in the depths. The waterfall looked like a sheet of blue **velour** as it swished down. Its edges were hemmed with whipped-white lines.

We could see a gaggle of **geese grazing** by the bank and the scene was picture perfect. A group of Amazonian ferns, edged with saw's teeth and statue still, added a tropical flavour. We stood under the waterfall to cool down, but it was catacomb cold. It gave us goose bumps immediately. We ended up **quivering** and shivering on the bank. The **nectar sweet smell** of the spring flowers perked up our spirits. We had a cup of chocolate and it was **Godlike** after our moment of madness.

LEVEL 4: ADVANCED PARAGRAPHS

We gasped in astonishment at the clarity of the **Caribbean-blue** waterfall. It was **spurting** over the basalt rock, spilling eel-like over the ledges. Its **clamorous** passage at the foot of the mountain threw up bubbles of spray. They sparkled uneasily in the dying light and shimmered like the ghostly, blood drops of a phantom.

There was a whooshing vortex at the bottom. It was caused by the **plummeting** funnel of water that spiralled from on high. It looked like a drape of **blue aluminium**, such was its lushness. The cascade was sieved with silver at its fringes, lending a hallucinatory quality to it.

Wagtails were bobbing and dipping on a rock, foraging for juicy flies. The tip of the rock pierced the **rhapsody-pool** like the upturned nose of a dwarf. Run off water tingled the rock as it seeped away, distilled as pure and clear as an angel's tears. There appeared to be a cave under the arch of waterfall. Quickly shedding our jumpers and shoes, the bravest of us plunged into it. The watery slide we passed through was so cold that our bodies were **quaking** when entering the cave.

At first, our only impressions were of a curtain of doom-black confronting us. Then our senses became fully attuned. The air was musty and rank, like sticking your head into an old dustbin. The reason why became obvious as our night vision kicked in. It was littered with fish bones, hundreds of them. Whether otter, heron or bear had done this over millennia, we did not know. The sooty darkness at the back of the cave seemed gloomy and dank and we felt that only impure, wicked things would be found there. None of us had the courage to delve any further. The bones seemed to grin up at our hesitation as we turned to go out.

We burst through the wall of water and looked up to see a hopeful, polestar-blue sky. A cup of hot soup was waiting for us and we sipped in silence. The fragrance of the **marzipan sweet** flowers added to the peace. It tasted **unearthly** and Arcadian after the experience of the cave. It gave a new meaning to the term comfort food.

LEVEL 5: COMPLEX WRITING: ROCK AND AWE

I ambled along the mountain path. An unusual humming sound vibrated in the air. It sounded like a swarm of bees. Then the buzzing transferred to the rock beneath my feet. It travelled through my body and I felt a tingle that ran up to my fingertips. I rounded the corner and the source of the sound revealed itself.

It was a whirruping waterfall. At this distance, it looked like silver tear tracks on the wrinkled face of the mountain. It was tiered and plunged into the depths of a paradise-blue pool. As I began to get closer, the noise of the cataract increased. It was growling and rumbling. Then it foamed into lather at the base. The waterfall seemed to fuse itself into distinct threads of watery fabric as I approached. It was as if a loom of liquid silver was pouring down the rocks. The sound was cacophonous now. The spout was hitting the cavernous hollow of the pool like a thunderclap. It rushed down the mountain, roiling and bubbling, boiling and churning. The pool fed two other smaller waterfalls, but they were not as deafening.

I walked along the edge of the rocks, leaving the swollen noise of the large pool behind. The sounds changed to a gentler swoosh-plunk and hiss-plop. It was still a salvo of sound, but it had a gentler slushiness to it. The two waterfalls streamed into one infinity pool of bliss. From it, the last spillway flowed, as smooth and fluvial as silver dew. It spilled over the gravelly bed with the honeyed sensuality of a lover's kiss. It was chiming as it slid, svelte and slinky, past my feet. The chinking, tinkling sound was caused by its languid slickness echoing from rock. It looked like the sleek robe of a water witch as its glassy brilliance pinged and plinked. Its edges were seamed in silver and glinted in the aureate light.

Just then, the sun came out. Its rays caught the watery slide, giving it a trance-like quality. It turned it a-glitter, like shreds of silky silver. The airy sparkling of its spray was magical. It looked like a spritz of fairy dust, flickering in the slanted light. It had the dreamy and illusory façade of a Renaissance painting and the same shimmering sorcery a mirage brings. The drizzling spray created a filmy mystique above the pool, dazzling me with its beauty. It gurgled from the depths and tinkled on the surface, swishing with a sylph-like melody.

The noise subsided as I walked away. It became a distant humming again. I ventured one look back over my shoulder. The willowy waterfall flashed silver one more time. Its soul-swelling magic followed me all the way home.

SIMILES

A **simile** is a comparison of two things using the words 'as' or 'like'. A comparison without those words would make it a metaphor again. A simile can be a highly effective tool when it is used properly. It is the 'silver bullet' in your armoury of literary techniques in many ways. This is because it enables a student to fuse two opposing or similar ideas into one sentence. That is the essence of figurative language and it can be the difference between a bland essay and a delightful one. Similes, just like metaphors, may range in complexity from a basic idea to higher ordered thinking.

A clear example of this is if you ask a mixed ability class to visualise a silver moon suspended over a calm sea. Then ask them to create the best simile they can to describe the moon's light. Assuming they have had some experience in using the book's formulas, you are likely to get an ascending order of thinking. It does not mean that the similes get any better. As I stated previously, in simplicity lies genius. It does mean, however, that the similes show more complexity as they move through the gears of thought. Underneath is an example.

1. Its beams hit the sea **like lines of silver fire**.
2. Its rays pierced the sea **like spears of glittering silver**.
3. Lances of light spilled across the sea **like silver tracers of fire.**
4. Its ghostly light shimmered on the water, silvering the sea **like rippling aluminium**.
5. The moons wraith-like light arrowed down **as eerily as a scene from an old fable**.
6. The moon's light was **as silver as diamond flame**, turning the sea a-glow **like melted platinum**.

It can be seen from the examples above that there are higher levels of thought evident in sentences four, five and six. It is debatable if they are more or less impactful than sentences one, two and three. It can be argued that the last three sentences are too long and cumbersome for a lot of readers. Both sets of sentences fulfil their main function, however. They merge and meld two opposing ideas into one sentence using 'as' or 'like'.

The final point is that similes are meant to be inventive. If, for example, a student was describing an old man, it would be rewarding if they could describe him in three similes like this: "The lines of life were written on his face **like a faded book**. Although his memories were **as cloudy as his eyes,** his desire to live burned **as bright as star flame**". It takes a lot of time, patience and practice to reach that economy of words with a student. Once they have mastered the art of the simile, they will knit their own beauty into the tapestry of writing. The ethereal beauty of an original simile enriches us all.

THE FOREST

COLOUR

LEVEL 1	LEVEL 2	LEVEL 3	LEVEL 4	LEVEL 5	OTHERS
bamboo-brown forest	teak-brown forest	conker-brown forest	umber-brown forest	mahogany-brown forest	
nut-brown forest	tannin-brown forest	oak-brown forest	beech-brown forest	almond-brown forest	

1. The bamboo-brown forest was a *leafy paradise*.
2. The teak-brown forest was a *woody heaven*.
3. The conker-brown forest was a *botanic wonderland*.
4. The beech-brown forest was a *sylvan Shangri la*.
5. The mahogany-brown forest was an *arboreal lotus land*.

SOUND

creaking trees	crinkly floor	clacking boughs	crackling leaves	rustling foliage	
crunching twigs	crispy grasses	crackly ferns	snapping branches	phut-phutting nuts	

1. The *aged* trees had creaking branches.
2. The *ancient* trees stretched away from the crinkly floor.
3. The *archaic* trees had clacking boughs and snapping branches.
4. The *arcane* limbs of the tree rustled and shook its crackling leaves.
5. The *antediluvian* trees dripped with delicious, phut-phutting nuts and berries.

METAPHORS

castles	high rises	fortresses	caretakers	sleeping souls	
towers	skyscrapers	citadels	guardians	pulsing	

| | | | | hearts | |

1. Trees are the castles of the **wood**.
2. Trees are the skyscrapers of the **glades**.
3. Trees are the citadels of the shady **groves**.
4. The sprawling trees are the caretakers of the **copses**.
5. The dendriform trees are the sleeping souls of the **thickets**.

ANIMAL SOUNDS OF THE FOREST

snuffling boar	scampering hares	screeching jays	shambling badgers	loping wolves	
slinking wildcats	scurrying squirrels	scuttling rabbits	skittering mice	lumbering bears	

1. Snuffling boar ate under **combs of feathery moss**.
2. Scurrying squirrels searched for food under **bristles of wispy moss**.
3. Scuttling rabbits played under **goatees of hanging moss**.
4. Shambling badgers rooted for food under **whiskers of whispering moss**.
5. Lumbering bears snorted and clawed under **beards of dripping moss**.

THE SHAPE OF STARS

luminous petals of silver	lucid snowflakes of silver	lambent asters of shiny silver	luminous pin pricks of glinting silver	lucent pentagrams of flashing silver	

1. Luminous petals of silver **freckled** the sky.
2. The stars were like lucid snowflakes of silver as they **sprinkled** the night sky.
3. The stars were like lambent asters of shiny silver as they **speckled** the night sky.
4. The night sky was **stippled** with stars, like luminous pin pricks of glinting silver.
5. The star-**studded** sky was flecked like lucent pentagrams of flashing silver.

EDIBLES OF THE FOREST

mushrooms	berries	wild basil	stinging nettle	plantain	
nuts	wood sorrel	wild garlic	chickweed	fairy ring champignon	

1. Mushrooms grew under the shady **roof** of the forest.
2. Berries lay ripening under the leafy **dome** of the forest.
3. Wild garlic dotted the floor under the **canopy** of the trees.
4. Chickweed flecked the ground under the **wreath** of leaves above.
5. Plantain sprouted up unannounced under the green **garland** of leaf and branch above.

OTHER IMAGES

moss-veiled trail	shady glades	clumps of moss	hoary boughs	leafy canopy	
leaf-carpeted path	reaching trees	secret groves	drumming woodpeckers	Jurassic ferns	

1. The moss-veiled trail snaked through the **care worn** forest.
2. The reaching trees were **time chiselled** and dying.
3. Clumps of moss swirled eerily from **toil worn** trees.
4. Drumming woodpeckers attacked the **wizened** bark of the trees.
5. The million-fold drip of rain sounded from the **world weary,** Jurassic ferns.

SENSATION

heart-warming	soul soothing	soul swelling	
heart comforting	soul nourishing	heart haunting	

1. The forest's beauty was heart-warming.
2. The wonder of the forest was soul nourishing.
3. The splendour of the forest was soul swelling.

SMELL

earthy	organic	mulchy	
pulpy	seasoned	loamy	

1. An earthy scent drifted towards our nostrils.
2. A seasoned smell wafted up from the forest's floor.
3. A loamy smell, rising up like a vent, drifted towards our nostrils.

TASTE

fruity	meadow sweet	trifle sweet	
orchard sweet	sherry sweet	mead sweet	

1. The wild berries tasted fruity.
2. The wild strawberries tasted sherry sweet.
3. The wild raspberries tasted trifle sweet to the palate.

LEVEL 1: BASIC SENTENCES

1. The forest was **nut-brown**. **COLOUR**
2. The twigs were **crunching** under my feet. **SOUND**
3. The trees were **the towers of the forest. METAPHOR**
4. I heard a **wildcat slinking** away. **ANIMAL SOUNDS**
5. The morning stars **shone like silver petals. THE STARS**
6. **Nuts** were scattered on the floor of the forest. **FOREST EDIBLES**
7. We took the **leaf-carpeted path** home. **OTHER IMAGES**
8. The beauty of the forest **comforted our hearts. SENSATION**
9. The smell of the forest was **pulpy. SMELL**
10. We picked some berries and they tasted **orchard sweet. TASTE**

LEVEL 2: A BASIC PARAGRAPH

The forest was **tannin-brown**. The grass was **crispy** under our feet. We looked up and the trees were **skyscraper tall**. Hares were **scampering** away from us up ahead. The morning stars were **shining like silver snowflakes**. **Wood sorrel** flecked the blanket of grass. We walked in and out of **shady glades**. The peace of the morning was **soul soothing**. The forest's smell was fresh and **organic**. We picked some wild pears and they were **meadow sweet**.

LEVEL 3: CREATIVE PARAGRAPHS

The forest we entered was **oak-brown** and primitive. The grasses we stepped on were **crackly** beneath our feet because of the recent dry spell. We were in awe of the size and majesty of the trees. Their knotted arms rose ever upwards, as far as my head could lift. They were **hoary fortresses** and stood proudly. The orchestra of birdsong we could hear from them suddenly stopped. A pair of **jays was screeching** high up in the canopy of the trees. Jays are the scavengers of the bird world. Their cruel, corvid eyes are always on the lookout for a feathered meal. In the winter, they raid squirrel stores for their nuts, often damning them to starvation. They drifted across our vision in a flash of flesh-pink and warlock-black, trying to size us up. That was the last we saw of them, as they are a furtive bird, full of suspicion. The morning stars peeped down at us **like silver asters**, glinting and shimmering. They looked happy in their solar-silver isolation. We could see **wild basil** growing freely on the **clumpy, mossy mattress** of the floor. The simpering wind carried a fragrance with it. It was **spirit refreshing to** smell the **mulchy mix** of the forest's perfume. We ate a few windfall apples and they were **mead sweet** with a bitter twist. It was only after we got the stomach cramps that we regretted it.

LEVEL 4: ADVANCED PARAGRAPHS

We were walking through an **umber-brown**, ancient forest. It reeked of age. Its woody incense was from centuries of **snapping branches** crashing to the forest's floor and rotting silently. The composting, organic smell rose up in waves like a miasma. Every sprawling tree we passed under reminded me of **a watchful guardian**, a silent sentinel of the groves. We decided to venture deeper into the tangled heart of this primeval forest. We hoped that it would reveal its dark secrets to us.

The further we went, the more mystical and spellbinding it became. Huge roots spread-eagled the ground, twisting like the great backs of sea dinosaurs. The foliage became thick and lush, forming an arch of fairytale-green above our heads. Arthritic boughs, gnarled with age, dripped their bounty of nuts onto the path. Briars, brambles and berry trees flanked the trail, making it impenetrable on either side. **Shuffling noises** came from deep in the interior, deadened by the cunningly woven web of leaves. A troupe of **shambling badgers** crossed the winding trail in front of us at one point. They were finishing up their early morning foraging and looked startled to see us.

We arrived at a wide glade, where the trees fell away, revealing the bespeckled sky. The last of the morning's stars were glinting **like silver pin pricks**, luminous and bright. An ore gold moon hung quietly in the distance, casting a honeyed sheen over the trees. We sat down with our backs against a lightning blasted tree trunk and watched it fade away. As if on cue, an avian aria erupted from the knot of trees. The solitary songbird was soon joined by his beaked companions, creating a symphony of song. The **heart haunting** melody was an elixir for the soul. The **sap sweet fragrance** of the forest washed over us and we were seduced by its comforting goodness. We placed some **stinging nettle leaves** into the broth we were brewing and it added a **tingling, chlorophyll** flavour. When we were leaving, I risked a glance over my shoulder. The forest glade looked freeze frame perfect in the enhanced light of the full dawn.

LEVEL 5: COMPLEX WRITING: THE ENCHANTED FOREST

The enchanted forest beckoned me into its pulsing heart. How could I resist such a lush Garden of Eden? The deep, haunting ballad of its ancient song called out to me. As old as Adam, the forest was still steeped in plushness and opulence.

With a light heart, I plunged into the over-arching vault of leaf and limb. It was not what I had expected. The exquisiteness of the dawn's light had not yet lanced to the lush, green sward. Because of this, hoods of black shadow hung in the groves.

Coils of vaporous mist enwrapped the shaggy heads of the oak trees. They writhed around them like a conjuror's milky smoke, sensuous and illusory. Sieves of mist caressed the lichen-encrusted bark. Adding its phantasmal gas to the damp breath of the forest, it glided with deadly intent. It deadened sound, haunted glades and poured into empty spaces. A sepulchral silence overhung the hallowed ground where the trees dared not grow. Nothing stirred, nothing shone, nothing sang. A hollow echoing, like the hushed tones of a great, slabbed cathedral, entombed the wood.

Then a finger of supernal light poked through the misty mesh. It was followed by a whole loom of light, filtering down in seams of gold. Like the luminal glow of the gods, it chased the shadows, banished the gloom and spilled into spaces where the mist once stalked. The fluty piping of a songbird split the silence just as the forest became flooded with light. A fusillade of trilling and warbling detonated all around me as the primordial forest came alive with the troubadours of the trees. I darted between shafts of lustrous-gold light as I went, admiring the butterflies. They pirouetted in the air, their wings a-whirr like little ripples of silk.

The glory of the forest was revealed in the birthstone-bright light. Almond-brown trees stood serenely, awash with a tender glow. Their bark looked like riffled toast and gems of amber clasped their crusty exterior. The first blush of the morn gave the leafy bower a green-going-to-gold complexion.

Idling past suede-soft flowers, I caressed them softly, getting tingles in my fingers. My ears perked up at the metallic, tinkling sound of a stream. It flashed with a tinsel tint through the lace of leaves. When the trees parted, I could see it was sliding into an infinity-pool. The pool looked like a polished mirror of silver, with skeins of swirl-white twisting slowly on the surface. A shiny spillway led to a choppier pond. Boulders colonized the edges of the pond, buffed with pillows of moss. They caused a rocky gurgling as water met stone; a swish, a clunk, a swell and a clop. Sweet fragrances, alluvial and palliative, seemed to flit in and out of my awareness. Sight and smell vied for attention in this soul-enriching dream world.

 I put my back against a knobbly boulder, leaning my head against the mossy pillow. I closed my eyes, let my stream of consciousness take hold, and drifted into infinity. When I awoke, I couldn't remember my dream, but softness and silvers still lingered in the memory of it.

PATHETIC FALLACY AND PERSONIFICATION

Pathetic fallacy is giving *inanimate* (non-living) nature human terms. This is the easiest definition of it, but there other rules to its use. It can also be used when **describing a character's mood in relation to the weather**. Sometimes it is better to pretend that it is called **'empathetic mistakes'** as this is, quite literally, its definition. If you think about it, giving non-living, naturally occurring objects any emotion is a big mistake! When it is used effectively, pathetic fallacy can breathe life into a passage and make a student's writing pleasant to the eye. Because the differences between pathetic fallacy and personification cause so much confusion, a grid system to help is below.

INANIMATE NATURE	WEATHER REFLECTING MOOD
The *river* was **babbling**.	The *doom-black sky* made the soldiers **fearful**.
The *mountains* were **brooding**.	The *wind howled* outside as the **orphans cried** within.
The *wind* was **moaning**.	The *radiant stars* made our **cares fall away**.
The *sun* was **staring** down at us.	The *sombre clouds* were **darkening our mood**.
The *moon* looked **lonely** in the sky.	The *heaving ocean* made us **feel ill**.

Personification is giving animate (living) nature, non-natural objects and ideas human terms. Personification can add a tantalising and thought-provoking dimension to your writing. The distinctions between this and pathetic are marginal, but they are there.

ANIMATE NATURE	NON-NATURAL OBJECTS
The *flowers* were **nodding their heads**.	The *ship* was **plodding** as it left the harbour.
The *lion* was **glaring** at me.	The *mobile phone* had a **mind** of its own.
The *bees* were **humming** a tune.	The *champagne glass* was pinging with **joy**.
The *trees* were **staring** at us.	The *car's engine* was screaming in **pain**.
The *blackbird* gave us an **aria**.	The *words* were **leaping** off the page.

PERSONIFYING IDEAS

Time is a great **healer**.
Fate was **hurrying** to meet me.
Destiny is no one's **slave**.
Courage is the **enemy** of weak men.
Cowardice is a strange **bedfellow** for a man.

LAKES

COLOUR

LEVEL 1	LEVEL 2	LEVEL 3	LEVEL 4	LEVEL 5	OTHERS
mirror-silver lakes	diamond flame-silver lakes	star fire-silver lakes	orris-silver lakes	verglas-silver lakes	
skyline-silver lakes	dew gleam-silver lakes	teardrop-silver lakes	argent-silver lakes	frazil-silver lakes	

1. The mountain's image was **stamped** onto the mirror-silver lake.
2. The mountain's reflection was **painted** onto the dew gleam-silver lake.
3. The mountain's reflection was **tattooed** onto the star fire-silver lake.
4. The reflection of the mountain was **minted** onto the orris-silver lake.
5. The mountain's likeness was **laminated** onto the frazil-silver lake.

THE SILENT VALLEY

cave quiet	convent quiet	nunnery quiet	cloister quiet	womb quiet	
cavern quiet	cathedral quiet	monastery quiet	confessional quiet	tomb quiet	

1. The **calm** lake was in the cavern quiet valley.
2. The **peaceful** lake was in the cathedral quiet vale.
3. The **placid** lake rested in the nunnery quiet glen.
4. The **serene** lake nestled in the cloister quiet gully.
5. The **becalmed** lake was in the bosom of the tomb quiet coombe.

THE CLEAR LAKE

window clear	gin clear	diamond clear	varnish clear	lacquer clear	

pane clear	vodka	decanter clear	veneer clear	moonshine clear	

1. The blue sky seemed to be *engraved* onto the pane clear lake.
2. The sky's image seemed to be *embedded* onto the gin clear lake.
3. The sky's reflection seemed to be *embalmed* onto the diamond clear lake.
4. The sky's sultry colour seemed to be *embossed* onto the varnish clear lake.
5. The sky's magnificence seemed to be *emblazoned* onto the lacquer clear lake.

THE STILL LAKE

statue still	yogi still	vault still	feng shui still	ossuary still	
shrine still	Buddha still	crypt still	Zen still	sarcophagus still	

1. The shrine still lake was *duck-pond round*.
2. The Buddha still lake was *fish-pond round*.
3. The crypt still lake was *reservoir round* and glittering.
4. The Zen still lake was *dew-pond round* and shimmering.
5. The ossuary still lake was *millpond round* and edged with tufty reeds.

FISH SOUNDS

bucking	thunking	flopping	plopping	plunking	
dive-bombing	plunging	flip-flopping	plip-plopping	ker-plunking	

1. Fish were bucking in the *glassy* lake.
2. Fish were plunging in the *glazed* lake.
3. Speckled fish were flip-flopping in the *crystalline* lake.
4. Dappled trout were plopping in the smooth, *vitreous* lake.
5. Colour-flecked fish were plunking in the beauteous, *hyaline* lake.

THE FLY ARMY

army	legion	squadron	platoon	brigade	
mob	division	regiment	phalanx	battalion	

1. An army of flies buzzed over the **hidden heart** of the lake.
2. A legion of flies droned over the **deep stomach** of the lake.
3. A regiment of insects hummed over the **confined womb** of the lake.
4. A platoon of midges hovered over the **measureless gullet** of the lake.
5. A battalion of insects swirled over the **fathomless bowels** of the lake.

A MOMENT OF CLARITY

an 'aha' moment	a light bulb moment	an eureka moment	an hosanna moment	an alleluia moment	
a 'zap' moment	a lightning bolt moment	an epiphany	a revelation moment	a hallelujah moment	

1. The **magic** of the lake caused an 'aha' moment.
2. The beauty and **witchcraft** of the lake caused a light bulb moment.
3. The naked **sorcery** of the lake gave me an epiphany.
4. The wonder and **thaumaturgy** of the lake caused a 'revelation moment'.
5. The mystique and **necromancy** of the lake brought a 'hallelujah moment' to my mind.

THE ISLAND IN THE LAKE

reed-fringed island	twisted trees	crumbling castle	gnarly bushes	stunted shrubbery	
quill shaped reeds	ruined walls	weather beaten boat	feral goats	lichen-encrusted rocks	

1. The **wind puffed** over the reed-fringed island.
2. The **wind breathed** over the twisted trees on the island.
3. The **wind exhaled** over the crumbling castle on the island.
4. The **wind sighed** gently over the gnarly bushes of the island.

5. The vernal *winds whispered* over the stunted shrubbery of the isle.

SENSATIONS OF PAIN

biting flies	stinging bees	nipping midges	
itching grass	pricking thistles	pinching ants	

1. The biting flies caused us to jump.
2. The stinging bees were painful.
3. The pinching ants caused us discomfort.

SMELL

sap sweet	nirvana sweet	saccharine sweet	
Eden sweet	utopia sweet	Zion sweet	

1. The wild roses smelled Eden sweet.
2. The crocuses on the waterfront smelled nirvana sweet.
3. The honeysuckle smelled Zion sweet.

TASTE

crisp water	spring fresh	crystalline taste	
glassy water	taste of sprite	tundra pure	

1. I took a drink from a lake stream. It tasted glassy and crisp.
2. It was spring fresh and sprightly.
3. It tasted crystalline and tundra pure, with an aftertaste of fresh sprite.

LEVEL 1: BASIC SENTENCES

1. The lake was skyline-silver. **COLOUR**
2. It lay in the middle of a cave quiet valley. **THE QUIET VALLEY**
3. It was window clear. **THE CLEAR LAKE**

4. It was peaceful and statue still. **THE STILL LAKE**

5. Trout were dive bombing in the lake. **SOUND**

6. A mob of flies rose into the air. **THE FLY ARMY**

7. I had a 'zap' moment because it was so beautiful. **A MOMENT OF CLARITY**

8. The itching grass snapped me out of it. **SENSATIONS OF PAIN**

9. A sap sweet smell hung in the air. **SMELL**

10. The water I drank was sharp but pleasant. **TASTE**

LEVEL 2: A BASIC PARAGRAPH

The lake was **as silver as diamond flame** and the atmosphere was **convent quiet**. Even the depths were **vodka clear**. It was soothing and **yogi still**. Freckled trout were leaping for flies and **thunking** on its surface. The rising sun caused **a division of armed flies** to swarm into the air. The scene was so glorious that I had **a lightning bolt moment**. The **thistles pricking** my leg broke my train of thought. The damp grass smelled **utopian**. I took a sip of water from a stream. It tasted like **a sweet medicine**, a potion for the spirit.

LEVEL 3: CREATIVE PARAGRAPHS

The lake appeared as if by magic as we crested the ridge. It was in **teardrop-silver** in colour and it was shaped like a perfectly flat disc of metal. No sound rang out from the shimmering emptiness of space around it. **Monastery quiet**, it was lined with pine trees and the whiff of mint wafted up to us. We decided to make our way to its **decanter clear** shore. The idyllic scene took our breath away. Unruffled by wind or rain, it was **vault still** and restful. The only sounds were the bumbling of bees and the heavy echo of a raven crawking.

Out on the lake, **flopping** trout were slapping the surface. They were hoping to catch one of the **squadron of flies** that buzzed about. The heaven-leaking light added a golden tint to the face of the lake and it was paradise. A startling **eureka moment** came unbidden, which involved the beauty of the natural world. I kept it to myself. The **nipping midges** didn't take away from the pleasure of that day. I can still see the rain-pearled grass in my mind's eye. I remember the **saccharine sweet** smell of that grass. I remember that the water **tasted like the nectar of the gods**. Most of all, I remember how it felt to be young on that special day.

LEVEL 4: ADVANCED PARAGRAPHS

The lake was glimmering in the callow light of dawn. Local legend had it that a giant hand had scooped out a gash of rock aeons ago. Then a great heap of **argent-silver** was moulded and poured into it, hemmed in by precipitous hills.

A broad span of Tuscany-blue sky was slashed above it, making it appear like nature's amphitheatre. The hollowness of the valley magnified all sounds, from burbling streams to the bumble of bees. The visage of the lake was **veneer-clear** and tranquil, flanked by avenues of cedar trees. There was **feng-shui** perfection to the scene, while the water was gilded with moonlight-pale lilies. **Plip-plopping** fish caused concentric rings to puff out and disappear as the air hummed all around us. **A phalanx of flies** was patrolling the water's edge, called into service by the heaven-filtering light.

Tolkein-esque ferns swayed beside a brook that spiralled down from a turf moor. The water had a peaty texture, but pools of molten gold lay naked in the light. At the bottom, smooth-edged stones glowed amber with a witchery uncommon to the modern world. I sat on a rock, admiring the glorious lustre of the water. The dingle became **confessional-quiet**. I had **an alleluia moment** then and yearned for a time when the world was young. A small thorn had **spiked** my foot, but it didn't break my reverie. The rain-winkled grass cast a silver sheen and the dewy air was laden with **cedar-sweet** smells. On impulse, I reached down and sipped from the stream. The taste was a mixture of rosewater and **chalybeate** that thrilled the tongue.

With a sigh, I got up forged my way homewards. It was a place with an eldritch beauty all of its own. I resolved to return one day to this halcyon paradise.

LEVEL 5: COMPLEX WRITING: THE BECALMED LAKE

I gazed upon the crumpled forehead of the mountain. It stabbed the clouds and loomed over me. It had a wizened and world weary aspect to it.

The first falls had made it snow snooded. A brooch of snow had clasped itself to the scalp of the mountain and it looked like the broken, jagged tooth of a hag. I could see the bare rock at the foot of it, however, as it hadn't been enwrought in wilderness-white yet. Where the mountain didn't block our view, the horizon was a perfect plumb line of pellucid-blue. A wing weary bird, sodden with the morning's dew, flashed across my vision and faded out of sight.

At eye level, a serene lake lay in front of us. It was **womb quiet** and **as clear as moonshine**. The wan sun had not scorched away the mist yet. It was as foul as a devil's broth, alien and otherworldly. It embalmed the space above the lake, rendering it **as quiet as a sarcophagus**. I sat down to wait for its brumous sheen to be burned away by the sun. Within the hour, its spirit-like form started to waver. It began to drift away, trailing at the lake with its gauzy claws. When its nebulous shimmering finally ceased, it transformed into wisps and vanished. The rain came then.

Like a druid's spittle, it was sibilant and stinging. It hissed and fizzed, boiling the surface of the lake, then subsided. When it ceased, lasers of light broke through the clouds. They criss-crossed the water in thin lines and drenched it with their brilliant beams. **A brigade of flies** rose up, quavering their wings and thrumming the air. Their little flitting's transformed into fluttery shadows on the **mere-silver water**. They couldn't affect the mountain's reflection at the edge of the lake. It seemed to be varnished onto it, like a glazed tattoo of elaborate beauty.

Only the occasional trout managed to explode its perfection. They were soaring up and **ker-plunking** down, causing mighty ripples which spiralled out to the island. The waves caused a twig to lollop in the water. Lichen-encased rocks gave the island its primeval quality, adding to the marvel of the occasion. I had **a hallelujah moment** then, a moment of clarity. I could see that the splendour of the world was inspired by a divine force. I realized that nature's sorcerous magic could salve the most oaken of hearts.

The **pinching ants** that clambered up my leg couldn't spoil the moment. A **Zion sweet smell** of heather and gorse percolated towards me. I cupped a handful of water in order to taste the bounty of this awe-inspiring lake. It was **tundra pure** to the tongue, just as I had expected. I feasted my eyes one last time on its transcendental beauty and made for home. It was a postcard-perfect vignette and I was sorry to leave it all behind.

EUPHONY

Euphony is using soft vowels, mellow consonants and pleasant words to create a soothing tone. In essence, it is the use of individual letters and phonics (vocal sounds) in order to recreate a harmony of sound in your writing. It is asking a lot to expect a student or child to incorporate this into their writing if they were not previously aware of it. It is another technique that requires time and patience. You will find, however, that they love working with soft sounds and soothing letters if it is approached in the right way.

For example, if you ask any child what the softest word in the English language is, they will struggle. If you ask them what word they would use to stop a child crying, they will immediately say **shush** or **hush**. You can then explain that the letters '**sh**' are the softest in the English language. A good exercise to try is to get them to write down what they think are the **softest letters** in the English language. If you agree with the letters, ask them to write down a list of soft sounding words containing those letters. Once they have ten words, ask them to put the words into a grid like the one below. That is a grid for a waterfall. Any soft sounds in nature, such as a river, birdsong or a gentle wind may be attempted. Those who do very well at this will most likely have a high degree of musical intelligence also.

The ability to use euphony in writing is a gift. That gift can be imparted by some simple exercises. If your students can make their words resonate like the glassy tinkle of a champagne flute, then that is a reward in itself for an educator.

WATERFALL GRID FOR EUPHONY

LETTERS	LEVEL 1	LEVEL 2	LEVEL 3	LEVEL 4	LEVEL 5
'sh'	swish	swoosh	lush	plush	swash
'll'	mellow	lullaby	illusory	allure	alleluia
'l'	loom	lilting	lithe	lyrical	lissome
'ee'	sheets	seeps	sleepy	sleepless	sheen
'm'	dreamy	ambrosial	mystical	melodious	mellifluous
'r'	swirls	suspires	murmurs	serene	luxurious
's'	whispers	blissful	slumbers	mystical	susurrous
'u'	azure	aura	mumbles	aurora	assuages
'w'	shallows	warblers	whish	whirrs	willowy
'zy'	hazy	dozy	gauzy	snoozy	wheezy

SPRING

COLOUR

LEVEL 1	LEVEL 2	LEVEL 3	LEVEL 4	LEVEL 5	OTHERS
pea-green fields	glade-green fields	mint-green fields	fairyland-green fields	paradise–green fields	
parsley-green fields	grape-green fields	malachite-green fields	fairytale–green fields	wonderland-green fields	

1. The pea-green fields were a *potion* for the soul.
2. The grape-green fields were a *balm* for the soul.
3. The mint-green fields were a gentle *salve* for the soul.
4. The sight of fairytale-green fields was like *manna* for my soul.
5. The sweeping vista of paradise-green was like a *lullaby* for my soul.

SOUND

bleating lambs	chirping chicks	yipping fox cubs	spluttering lawnmowers	palpitating heart of	
lowing calves	crooning pigeons	whinnying foals	snipping shears	throbbing heart of	

1. Bleating lambs were playing on the *ripe* grass.
2. Crooning pigeons plucked for seeds on the *juicy* grass.
3. Whinnying foals frolicked and frisked on the *lush* grass.
4. Spluttering lawnmowers whittled and sheared the *plush* grass.
5. The throbbing heart of nature beat rhythmically under the *succulent* grass.

SIMILES FOR THE MOON

like a shimmering disc	like a gleaming globe	like a glowing orb	like a shiny salver	as freshly-minted as a coin	

1. The spring moon *hung* in the sky like a shimmering disc of silver.

2. The moon *hovered* in the sky like a gleaming globe of gold.

3. The moon *lingered* in the sky like a glowing orb of gold.

4. The moon *loitered* in the night sky like a shiny salver of silver.

5. The moon *languished* in the night sky. It seemed as freshly-minted as a silver coin.

THE MOVEMENT OF SCENTS

blew	drifted	glided	puffed	swirled	
carried	floated	hovered	percolated	drafted	

1. The *pure*, spring smells carried to me.

2. The *sparkling*, spring scents drifted towards me.

3. The *chaste*, spring aromas glided to my nose.

4. The *sanitizing*, spring fragrances percolated around the glade.

5. The *salubrious*, spring perfumes drafted and swirled from the flowers.

SPRING FLOWERS

daisies	dandelions	peonies	primroses	daffodils	
buttercups	tulips	crocuses	honeysuckle	bluebells	

1. The buttercups *grew* on the green grass.

2. The dandelions *sprung up* from the verdant grass.

3. The peonies *sprouted* from the verdure of the grass.

4. The primroses *burst forth* from the virescent grass.

5. Bluebells *exploded* from the verdurous robe of the grove.

METAPHORS FOR THIN LIGHT

strings	staffs	arrows	ribbons	lasers	
strands	shafts	spears	fingers	lances	

1. *Thin* strings of light came from the sky.

2. **Slim** shafts of light came from the sky.

3. Arrows of **lean** light filled the sky.

4. **Slender** ribbons of light swooped down from the firmament of the sky.

5. **Tapered** lances of light descended from the empyrean vault above.

OTHER IMAGES

splay-legged lambs	open-beaked chicks	misty-eyed fox cubs	turtle-snow lawnmowers	turbo-winged blackbirds	
milk-splashed calves	proud-breasted pigeons	star-blazed foals	scalpel-sharp shears	yolk-yellow ducklings	

1. Splay-legged lambs played under the **shiny frame** of sky.

2. Open-beaked chicks twittered under the **silk canvas** of sky.

3. Star-blazed foals pranced under the **satin ceiling** of sky.

4. Turtle-slow lawnmowers snipped grass under the **glossy screen** of sky.

5. Turbo-winged blackbirds whirred under the **velvety easel** of sky.

SENSATION

cool	soothing	caressing	
pleasant	salving	ruffling	

1. The winds were cool and pleasant.

2. The spring winds were soothing to the touch.

3. The vernal winds were caressing my face and ruffling my hair.

SMELL

baked apple	candied	confectionery	
cream sweet	caramel	tutti-frutti	

1. The baked apple smell of the meadow was pleasant.

2. The meadow had a candied aroma. It smelt like fragrant caramel.

3. The tutti-frutti scent of the meadows and vales was overpowering.

TASTE

| floral | petal sweet | molasses sweet | |
| candy floss sweet | blossom sweet | meringue sweet | |

1. The wild thyme we picked was floral to the taste.

2. The ramsons we plucked were petal sweet to the taste.

3. The chanterelles we picked were meringue sweet.

LEVEL 1: BASIC SENTENCES

1. The fields were **parsley-green**. **COLOUR**

2. Lonely calves were **lowing** in the fields. **SOUND**

3. The moon was **like a ghostly-silver disc** in the sky. **SIMILES FOR THE MOON**

4. A carnival of **scents blew** in the air. **THE MOVEMENT OF SCENTS**

5. A **host of daisies** scattered the meadow. **SPRING FLOWERS**

6. **Strands of thin light** came from the sky. **METAPHORS FOR LIGHT**

7. The **milk-splashed calves** brayed for company. **OTHER IMAGES**

8. The scene was **spirit-lifting**. **SENSATION**

9. There was a **cream fresh** smell. **SMELL**

10. The spring foods had a **candy floss sweet** taste. **TASTE**

LEVEL 2: A BASIC PARAGRAPH

The fields were **glade-green**. The sound of **chirping chicks** filled the air. The moon was **like a phantom-silver orb**. A pageant of **smells floated** in the spring air and a horde of **dandelions** littered the meadow. **Staffs of slim light** spilled from the sky. **Proud-breasted pigeons** strutted across the meadow. The scene was **spirit-refreshing** and pastoral. The meadow smelled **pear fresh**. There was a **blossom sweet** taste to the food we ate.

LEVEL 3: CREATIVE PARAGRAPHS

The **malachite-green** fields seemed to be covered in a bright sheen under the dawn moon. We could hear **yipping fox cubs** breaking the quiet of the world. Clouds shaped like tufty pillows glided slowly across the sky. They carried an airy, warm, drizzling rain with them. It cleansed the land and banished the strangling coldness and stunned silence of winter. Plinking and pattering off the leaves, then fading into memory, the rain energized the flora. It left behind a world baptized and rebirthed by its liquid grace. Song thrushes trilled as the **spectre-silver moon** began to wane and the fog of flowers in the meadow slowly revealed itself. We could smell their **aromas hovering** in the air.

Versace-purple crocuses seemed to glow before our eyes. Jewel-green grasshoppers bounced atop the grass like leggy trampolines. In the stony verges, Rafael-red valerian sprouted from between coral-black cracks. **Spears of dawn light** suddenly drenched the farthest corners with their golden magic. A pair of **misty-eyed cubs** yelped as they saw us and darted to safety. A murmuration of starlings wheeled and banked overhead like wind-tossed gunpowder. The rustic scene was **spirit-renewing** and we let the menu of **melon fresh scents** wash over us. We ate our hamper of food under the leafy umbrella of a great oak and it tasted **molasses sweet**.

LEVEL 4: ADVANCED PARAGRAPHS

The dawn chorus is the herald of spring. It starts with a lonely, serenading minstrel, usually a blackbird. He is clear and melodious, as fresh and sweet as the gardens he will later raid. In the neighbouring tree, his future ex-wife trumpets a fluty duet. Her saucy fanfare dares others to match their salsa song of the canopy. The competition rouses from their slumber, opening their beaks to the heavens. The avian aria slowly becomes a fugue, bouncing through bough and bower. The lilting majesty of their song cascades into open spaces, through glassy windows, and onto the smiling lips of the dreamers within. Spring is here.

What are the triggers for the comforting cannon of tree music? Is it the lace of morning fog slowly receding as the months roll by? Is it the gently unfurling flowers, velour soft and receptive to warmth? Is it the baked oven smell of grass as the sun purges it of water? It is this and more. It is the world moving from iron-grey to fairyland –green. It is the spools of lambs' wool hanging from straggly bushes, a wedding card to the nesters. It is the mist of smells, the frill of flowers and the scent of magic in the air. Shoals of honeysuckle, primroses and bluebells sway and weave a rich mosaic in the meadows. Harp strings of golden light touch steaming shadows and soften the frozen earth for the wildflowers. Turtle-slow lawnmowers pedicure the grass, while leaving their clippings behind for the fussy nesters. Gnarled hands with snipping shears scalp the hedges. The world is young, lush and bountiful again. It is a spirit-enriching, pastoral scene. Under the wraith-silver moon, an alchemy of balsamic scents swirl around the meadow. Human foods become peach sweet to the taste after the scavenging fangs of winter turned them tasteless.

What of the dreamers? The same, easy smile plays on their lips. They are listening to the theatre of the trees while they sleep. To them, it is a song woven from lilting lullaby and brazen beak. They do not know that it is an ode older than the span of man's dreams. They may never see the beauty of the brood-mance of the bower. Neither the finest pane of daylight nor the most cunning tint of moonlight shall match the opus of the dawn chorus. Spring is here.

LEVEL 5: COMPLEX WRITING: SPRINKLING STARDUST

Spring is glee. It's a fizzy tonic, like a slowly overflowing bottle of bubbling joy. It tattoos its colours onto the land, banishing the clay-cold claws of winter. The blessed dew is bespangled on the frosty ground. Like wizard dust, it burns the snow into oblivion. Buds blossom, trees thaw and grass grows. Spring cauterizes, with a surgical precision, the gaping wounds winter leaves on the land. When it's finished, it infuses its own mojo into the endless opera of the seasons.

One fine morning, the world wakes up to a rapture-blue sky. It is high and bright, a continuum of delight that salves both spirit and soul. The grass becomes wonderland-green as if some magical jujitsu chop has banished the frost overnight. Squillions of glint-silver dewdrops are sprinkled in the meadow like stardust. They are shimmering Eden pills that signal to the grass it's time to revive. Like slinky escapologists, the seeds below slip through the iron shackles of the earth. Finally, flowers begin to wave at the ecstasy-blue sky again. Within days, cherry blossoms are manicured with bliss-pink petals.

Splay-legged lambs, acolyte-white in colour, wobble on their knobbly joints before going a-gambol in the fields. Waves of coruscating light immerse the meadows in sheets of golden flame. Bluebells and daffodils add to the stained-glass perfection of the forest's colours. Tufty thickets burst forth as everything is a-tangle in the branches for birdy kiss-and-tells. Little feathers mysteriously appear under conker-brown trees.

Spring is here. It is the time of the 'lings; nestlings, seedlings and ding-a-lings. In finely woven nests, tiny hearts tap with joy. Under the ground, shoots shaped like tadpoles replace crusty bulbs. The first bike-racers appear, zinging down country lanes, terrorizing baby hedgehogs. Overhead, an exodus of banished birds appears as if out of a Celtic fairytale.

Honking geese and whooping swans are joined by the sinister cuckoo. To-whom-do-you-brood-with is his sorrowful call and the answer will doom some of the nestlings.

In the distance, the world's greatest sound is coming out of hibernation. It is the mellifluous hum of a distant lawnmower, signalling that the land is warm again. Its distant drone is a sort of surrogate wind music, flowing into winter-battered ears. Whittling and shearing the grass to perfection, it provides symmetry to winter's jumble sale of chaos. The air smells like baked sugar cakes after the grass is shorn. Snowmelt makes the rivers pulse like wondrous veins. They surge to collect winter's clutter, rumbling through rocky channels.

Thumb-plump bumblebees, wings a-thrum, loot from honeypots of mustard-yellow flowers. They sound like mini tumble dryers, plunging syringe-like to extract their booty. Nickering foals prance and cavort in carnival-green fields. The pumping heart of nature is beating again. Spring is nature's defibrillator, a high voltage pacemaker that jump starts life into the land. It throbs and thumps to its own high octane rhythm and composes its own symphony of sound. It has a life, a fragrance and a lilting synergy unique to itself. If it were a perfume, it would be called eau-de-Glee.

*Type '**Describing a garden in spring**' into Google for another post relevant to this genre. It will come up on the '**Best Descriptive Websites**' blog post at: www.descriptivewriting.wordpress.com.

ALLITERATION

Alliteration occurs when words start with the same sound. This is usually taken as consonant sounds in modern literature, but it includes vowel sounds also. It is important to note that the letters do not need to be the same at the start of the word; it is the sound that is important. Alliteration is one of the main literary devices employed by writers and poets to make a sentence or phrase more memorable. That is why it is a mnemonic device. A mnemonic device, to use a metaphor for it, is a **'mental hook'** for the reader.

Teaching students how to understand and use alliteration in their writing is always interesting. The best way of approaching the issue is to ask them to recite a nursery rhyme. It truly is astonishing how many of us can recite nursery rhymes, some of which are centuries old. Why are nursery rhymes so easy to recite and remember? The answer is that they are a pulsating, throbbing, vibrant mnemonic device. They all share the same qualities of alliteration, repetition, assonance, onomatopoeia and end rhyme. For example, '**R**ing-a –**r**ing o' **R**oses' and '**B**aa, **b**aa, **b**lack sheep' are both thought to date to the eighteenth century in written form, but were almost certainly constructed at least three hundred years earlier. So how did they survive in oral form only for those two hundred years?

It is significant that the opening sentences are alliterative as this would appeal to a child. Using alliteration in a writing composition has the same effect. When a reader comes across a 'catchy' sentence, it tends to linger in the memory instead of fading. By using alliteration, a student is adding to the armoury of devices he has at his disposal. It should always be encouraged, but there is a word of caution attached to its use. It should never be over used as this can make the passage of writing seem too contrived and cumbersome to read. Two or three examples per passage of writing are fine. Underneath are some examples of alliteration.

1. The *c*hoir of birds looked *k*ingly and *k*ind.
2. I *d*rank *d*eep from the stream and it was *d*elightful.
3. The *s*weet *s*cent was a merely a *s*ilent *s*uspicion in the air.
4. The *c*rows were *c*awing in their *c*ruel and *c*unning voices.
5. The *b*each was *b*irthstone-*b*irth and the sand gleamed like *b*ejewelled dust.

SUMMER

COLOUR

LEVEL 1	LEVEL 2	LEVEL 3	LEVEL 4	LEVEL 5	OTHERS
plum-purple skies	juniper-purple sunsets	amethyst-purple dusk skies	orpine-purple night skies	monarchy-purple sunrises	
heather-purple skies	mulberry-purple sunsets	magenta-purple dusk skies	Tyrian-purple night skies	royal-purple gloaming	

1. The *close of day* brings plum-purple skies.
2. The summer *dusk* brings mulberry-purple skies.
3. The summer *twilight* brings glorious, magenta-purple skies.
4. The *gloaming* of the night gathers up the orpine-purple skies.
5. The *crepuscular* light heralds the onset of the monarchy-purple skies.

BEE MUSIC

buzzing bees	droning bees	mumbling bees	the murmuration of bees	cult hum of bees	
humming bees	intoning bees	murmuring of bees	the mussitation of bees	monk hum of bees	

1. The buzzing bees sound like *electric shavers*.
2. The droning bees sound like dozy *lawn mowers*.
3. The mumbling of bees sounds like *buzz saws* cranking up.
4. The orinasal murmuration of bees sounds like *hairdryers* flying in the sky.
5. The monk-hum of plump, banded bees is like the start of a *Formula One* race.

METAPHORS FOR THE SUN

a dazzling circle	a flashing fireball	a glittering eye	a flaming wheel	a fiery ring	
of chrome-gold	of magma-red	of luminous-gold	of saffron-orange	of lava-red	

1. The sun is a dazzling circle of gold in the **sweep of sky**.
2. The sun is a flashing fireball of magma-red in the **large expanse** of sky.
3. The sun is a glittering eye of luminous-gold in the **great spread** of sky.
4. The sun is a flaming wheel of saffron-orange in the **vast scope** of sky.
5. The sun is a fiery ring of lava-red in the **vast span** of sky.

THE DAWN CHORUS

a beaked concert	a feathered melody	an avian aria	a carolling opera	a winged symphony	
a beaked chorus	a feathered medley	an ancient alchemy of song	a quavering orchestra	a winged sorcery	

1. The beaked concert came from the **pop stars** of the trees.
2. The feathered melody came from the **musicians** of the trees.
3. The avian aria came from the **carollers** of the trees.
4. A quavering orchestra came from the **minstrels** of the trees.
5. A winged symphony erupted from the **troubadours** of the trees.

EDIBLE FOODS

wild thyme	ramsons	bilberry	chanterelles	giant puffball	
cep	shaggy ink cap	black mustard	sweet violet	parasol mushroom	

1. Wild thyme forms a **blanket** in the forest.
2. Shaggy ink cap forms a rich **carpet** on grassy verges.

3. Black mustard adds to the colourful **duvet** of colour.

4. Sweet violet litters the mossy **mattress** of the forest.

5. Parasol mushrooms seem woven into the floral **quilt** of floor.

THE SWEEP OF SKY

endless	eternal	everlasting	measureless	limitless	
unending	infinite	perpetual	immeasurable	boundless	

1. The clouds seem **bolted** to the endless sky.

2. The clouds seem **yoked** to the infinite sky.

3. The flimsy clouds seem **riveted** to the everlasting skies.

4. The fleecy clouds seem **shackled** to the measureless skies of summer.

5. The tufty clouds seem **manacled** to the limitless skies of summer.

THE BRIGHEST BLUES

chemical-blue skies	solar-blue skies	electric-blue skies	polaris-blue skies	celestial-blue skies	
cocktail-blue skies	brochure-blue skies	neon-blue skies	plasma-blue skies	constellation-blue skies	

1. The sky becomes a **dome** of chemical-blue.

2. The sky becomes a **shrine** of brochure-blue.

3. The sky transforms into a **temple** of electric-blue.

4. The summer sky morphs into a **cathedral** of plasma-blue.

5. The ravishing sky of summer merges into one, great **pantheon** of celestial-blue.

SENSATIONS

feather soft	cotton soft	silk soft	
downy soft	eider soft	velvet soft	

1. The grass was feather soft.

2. The grass was eider soft, the texture of cotton.

3. The lush, summer grass was velvet soft to the touch.

SMELL

a soup of smells	a broth of smells	a goulash of smells	
a stew of smells	a brew of smells	a buffet of smells	

1. A soup of smells came from the corn fields.
2. A brew of smells came from the golden, wheat fields.
3. A buffet of smells emanated from the wholesome, barley fields.

TASTE

lozenge sweet	honeysuckle sweet	marzipan sweet	
gelatin sweet	citrus sweet	manna sweet	

1. The summer apples were lozenge sweet.
2. The summer pears were citrus sweet and delectable.
3. The bumper summer harvest was manna sent and had a faint hint of marzipan.

LEVEL 1: BASIC SENTENCES

1. The night sky was **heather-purple**. **COLOUR**
2. **Humming bees** darted through the air. **BEE MUSIC**
3. The stars were **glittering like scattered space dust**. **METAPHORS FOR THE SUN**
4. The **beaked chorus** of birds filled the air. **THE DAWN CHORUS**
5. The edible **ceps** looked like shiny penny buns. **EDIBLE FOODS**
6. Clouds were latched to the **unending sky**. **THE SWEEP OF SKY**
7. The afternoon sky was **cocktail-blue**. **THE BRIGHTEST BLUES**
8. The grass was **downy soft**. **SENSATION**
9. **A stew of smells** filled the air. **SMELL**
10. The summer food was **gelatin sweet**. **TASTE**

LEVEL 2: A BASIC PARAGRAPH

The night sky was **juniper-purple**. The sound of **intoning bees** filled the air. The **stars were glowing like beacons** for the lost souls of the world. A **feathered medley** echoed through the trees. The garlic smell of **ramsons** drifted through the air. The clouds were bracketed to the **eternal, summer** sky. It was like a dome of **solar blue**. The grass was **silk soft**. **A broth of smells** swirled around me. The food we ate was **honeysuckle sweet**.

LEVEL 3: CREATIVE PARAGRAPHS

An **amethyst-purple** tint invades the late summer skies. The world is changing and autumn is approaching. Soon the land will be a-fire in the warm glow of tree-flame. Pagan rituals such as Hallowe'en will bring back long dead memories of trolls, spooks and hobgoblins. For now, however, the fields are still Elysium-green. Bees are still murmuring in that strange **cult hum** exclusive to them. They flit from flower to flower, surfing the short spaces as they go. The stars are summer stars, **flickering like pulsing lodestars**. A sol-fa of song erupts as they fade away, the **ancient alchemy of the dawn chorus**.

Bilberries and chanterelles adorn the forest floor, questing for sunlight. **The perpetual skies of summer** are buckled with clouds and they flare up in a luminous, **neon-blue** when the mood takes them. Summer is nature's treasure trove. The fields are laden with goldenrod-yellow flowers and silver-washed fritillaries carry their bushels of pollen carefully. **A goulash of scents** twirls above the **satin soft petals** and the **pear sweet taste** of the air is a blessed joy.

But summer brings with it a bitter twist. The nights are closing in on each other and the long days are faltering. Enjoy the beaches, the barbecues and the birds. In a few short months, all will be cold.

LEVEL 4: ADVANCED PARAGRAPHS

Water, water, everywhere and not a drop to drink. I am doomed.

The wooden planks of flotsam I have cobbled together after the shipwreck are coming loose. I am sitting on a floating coffin with makeshift oars. It's like Satan's sauna out here in this big, blue tomb. The emptiness in my soul matches the spiritless sky and the featureless waterscape around me.

The days are the worst. The remorseless sun bends his full will against my survival and he is winning. I feel like I have been stabbed by a million sun spears. My blood simmers, my brain stews, and even my bones seem to smoulder in their meaty carcass. Dead man drifting. That's who I am. I am floundering in a sea of divine-blue quicklime and there's no escape. My tongue feels like a slab of lead, cloven to the roof of my mouth. My throat is parched and my lips are chapped and flaky. Only a god could save me now.

Below the surface, huge shapes glide. Their fins break the surface like steel triangles, leaving barely a ripple. They circle and circle, constantly searching for weakness. They have followed me for three days and nights, cruel and cunning as they are. The knife fixed to the end of the oar can only keep them at bay for so long.

The tides are the mistress of the sea. They dictate the level of wind necessary for my forward movement. No tides, no wind, no survive. That's why I hate the nights. A vast shroud of Barabbas –black fills the abyss of sky above. The wind dies down as the eerie, spectral moon appears. It casts down splinters of Solomon-gold, making the sea crests sparkle like elf-light. It is merely an illusion of beauty. I can see the full glitter of their beady eyes and the flash of their scalpel sharp teeth as they grin at me. The only sounds to keep me company are the sigh of wind, the slap of oar and the slosh of wave. The leavening sea is my enemy. It is as cold as a ghoul's soul and my teeth are rattling and chattering. The haunting cheep-cheep of a passing tern reminds me how powerless I really am. Even he can go home. The stink of a thousand seas surrounds me. It is a mix of rotting kelp and dying fish. It assaults my nostrils and steals my hope.

But lo! There's a huge magma-red light in the distance. I am rocked by a huge wave which pushes me towards the light. All the gods are with me. My name is Lucius Andropedus. I am a fisherman from Pompeii and I am lost at sea. It is The Year of Our Lord 79 A.D, somewhere off the coast of Italy, and I am saved.

LEVEL 5: COMPLEX WRITING: SEA MUSIC

The cliff we stood on seemed as old as Abraham. Far below, the hungry sea gnawed at its ankle.

Someone once said that paradise is where seagulls are flying beneath your feet. They were arcing and wheeling between the witchcraft of the morning light. An occasional scream would echo from the cliffs, eerie and resonating. The immense vista leading to the horizon was jaw dropping. The Prussian-blue vault of velvet above seemed to solder into the liquid blanket of silver beneath. Far out to sea, a solitary cormorant, sleek wings a-flurry, streaked out to the place where sea and sky melt into each other and was lost from sight.

The slurpy slapping of the sea was muted, a metronomic murmur. The waves were merely snoozing, sluggish and slumbering in their liquid robes. They dribbled up to the beach of the sheltered cove, then shuddered and drizzled their sea spray onto its surface, whisking the stones before releasing. A current of cold electricity passed through the air. We shivered. The wind whipped up. The sea simmered.

Sloshing, swollen to its confined depths, its cavernous bowels stirred, a growling from the fathoms. Suddenly, stone dashed sand teemed as the sea hissed, washed, polished, and lashed the pebbles before sloshing back. It hissed, slipped, dashed the sand and released; fizzed, spit, seethed the beach and released: sizzed, slapped, swished the stones and released.

The mesmeric beauty of its beat was heart-swelling. We realized then that the sea was its own master, kindling its own symphony. It hadn't finished its song yet, however. The wind, the midwife of the seas, served a different master and whipped it into a frenzy.

The echo of a raspy rumbling from the enraged sea came to us, a tremulousness to fear. The waves were really sloshing, slurping and slobbering with their salty lips. They pounded into the cliff of the sheltered cove, then paused and pounced with malice onto its ankle, slamming the rock before releasing. A rumour of its malevolence passed through our legs. We shivered. The wind died down. The sea bubbled. Trembling, throbbing to its rotten beat, its malicious soul stirred, a warning from the ages. Suddenly, rip-tide rolls heaved as the sea foamed, crashed, pounded and bashed the cliff-foot before sloshing back. It foamed and frothed, plunged down hard and pummelled the hated cliffs; it lathered and lacerated, bucked waves and buckled itself; it smacked and smashed, surging waves and expunging its awful rage.

Its hissy fit over, it swelled once more, juddered and was still.

ARCHAIC WORDS

An archaic word is an old word from a previous era, one that is no longer in common use. Using an archaic word in a passage of writing adds an alien glamour to it. It is particularly appropriate to use it when writing about autumn, the mist and medieval battle scenes. Autumn is a season that has a resonance all of its own. In order to truly catch its essence, words like a-flame, eldritch and aeons should be used. That is because autumn reminds us of the **atavistic pulse**. This is my phrase for the memories we have built into our DNA of collecting hazelnuts, picking blackberries and fishing for salmon. Traces of those memories still exist, to a lesser or larger degree, in most of us.

Similarly, the mist has a fey and primeval quality to it that cannot be compared to any other aspect of nature. It can glow with an unearthly sheen or it can obscure whole forests and meadows with its otherworldly veil of grey. Medieval battle scenes are a great way to encourage the use of archaic words also. It is my experience that students love the texture and primeval feel of words such as **jousting** knights, **argent**-silver armour and **caterwauling** cries. A good suggestion is to get them to keep a 'new vocabulary' notebook, as I do. They can then keep a special section at the back of it for archaic words. The definition of the archaic words may be written in as they come across them. Using archaic words will give any passage of writing the atavistic and primordial quality needed to make it unique.

'EN' ARCHAIC WORDS	'BE' ARCHAIC WORDS	OTHERS TO USE
enclad	beclouded	comely
enkindled	bedecked	gloaming
enmeshed	bedewed	to mar
enraptured	bedimmed	nethermost
enshrouded	bedizened	to quaff
ensnared	begilt	riven
entombed	begirded	to smite
entwined	benighted	sward
enwrapped	bespangled	trove
enwrought	bespeckled	days of yore

AUTUMN

COLOUR

LEVEL 1	LEVEL 2	LEVEL 3	LEVEL 4	LEVEL 5	OTHERS
lava-red leaves	magma-red leaves	bonfire-red leaves	inferno-red leaves	pyre-red leaves	
ember-red leaves	molten-red leaves	barbecue-red leaves	incinerator-red leaves	conflagration-red leaves	

1. The lava-red leaves are an **omen** of bad weather ahead.
2. The magma-red leaves are an **oracle** for bad weather ahead.
3. The bonfire-red leaves are like an **augury** of doom.
4. The inferno-red dome of leaves is a **portent** that winter is nigh.
5. The pyre-red canopy is a **harbinger** for the scavenging skies of winter to appear.

UNUSUAL WIND SOUNDS

the nuzzling winds	the ruffling winds	the kneading winds	the soughing winds	the wheezing winds	
the huffing winds	the yawning winds	the muffling winds	the suspiring winds	the whisking winds	

1. The wind was nuzzling the **blood-red** leaves.
2. The ruffling winds were scattering the **bold-red** leaves.
3. The kneading breezes fluttered the **saucy-red** leaves.
4. The soughing winds moaned through the **crucifixion-red** leaves.
5. The whisking wind was tousling the **stigmata-red** leaves.

METAPHORS FOR THE CLOUDS

airy anvils	cosmic	smoky	heavenly	steamy	

	cloaks	shields	hoods	shrouds	
puffy plates	fluffy fleeces	billowy bells	puffing palls	vaporous veils	

1. The clouds **drift** like airy anvils.
2. The clouds **float** like cosmic cloaks.
3. The autumn clouds **glide** like smoky shields.
4. The misty clouds **sail** like heavenly hoods.
5. The diaphanous clouds **skim** across the sky like steamy shrouds.

ARCHAIC WORDS FOR AUTUMN

leaves a-fire	trees a-flash	oak leaves a-light	leafy dome a-glow	canopy a-scorch	
leaves a-flame	trees a-flicker	ash trees a-blaze	leafy arch a-gleam	sessile canopy a-smoulder	

1. The trees are a-fire in a **patchwork** of colour.
2. The trees are a-flash in a **collage** of colour.
3. The trees are a-blaze in a **tapestry** of vivid colour.
4. The age old trees are a-glow in a **mosaic** of colour.
5. The primeval trees are a-scorch in a **brocade** of colour.

AN AUTUMN FEAST

slurping on blackberries	drooling over strawberries	slobbering on elderberries	munching on wild apples	crunching on hazelnuts	
chomping on blackcurrants	gulping on gooseberries	dribbling over sloe berries	gorging on sweet chestnut	masticating on walnuts	

1. We enjoyed slurping on blackberries under a **crescent moon**.
2. We loved drooling over strawberries under a **gibbous moon**.
3. We had fun dribbling over sloe berries under a **harvest moon**.

4. We were munching on wild apples under a **hunter's moon**.

5. We were crunching on the hazelnuts under the full light of a **moth-moon**.

COLOURS USING HEAT

hot-reds	burning-browns	glowing-golds	feverish-yellows	broiling-oranges	
fiery-reds	blazing-browns	smouldering-golds	scorching-yellows	sweltering-oranges	

1. The hot-reds give the trees a strange **glamour**.

2. The burning-browns cast an alien **charm** over the trees.

3. The glowing-golds spill an arcane **hex** over the trees.

4. The scorching-yellows are a **self-exorcism** of the pastel colours.

5. The broiling-oranges are a chemical **self-immolation** before the winter sets in.

OTHER IMAGES FOR AUTUMN

ghost-grey skies	owls hoot	rain drenches people	ghostly cords of moonlight	listless ligaments of light	
ghoul-grey skies	owls haunt	rain douses people	eerie tendrils of moonlight	the straining light of autumn	

1. The ghoul-grey skies of autumn **stare** down on us.

2. Owls hoot and haunt the night, flitting through trees like **vengeful** phantoms.

3. Sun and rain douses people equally with the strange, **schizophrenic** weather of autumn.

4. Ghostly chords of moonlight creep from trees with the phosphorescent glow of the **supernatural**.

5. Scimitar-winged swallows return home to Africa, framed by the straining, **voodoo** light of autumn.

SENSATION

nervous	spooked	unhinged	
afraid	daunted	unmanned	

1. The eerie autumn light made us nervous.
2. The taboo customs of Hallowe'en spooked us.
3. The ghostly magic of autumn's gloaming unmanned us.

SMELL

a menu of scents	a perfumery of scents	a scullery of scents	
a larder of aromas	a pot-pourri of aromas	a smorgasbord of smells	

1. A menu of scents came from our berry basket.
2. The chrysalis-silver moon seemed to magnify the pot-pourri of aromas swirling in the forest.
3. The luchre-gold light of the moon seemed to accentuate the smorgasbord of smells in the forest.

TASTE

a savoury taste	a ravishing taste	a wholesome taste	
a mouth-watering taste	an exquisite taste	a toothsome treat	

1. The wild elderberries had a mouth-watering taste.
2. The hazelnuts dipped in honey had an exquisite taste.
3. The walnuts dipped in cream were a toothsome treat.

LEVEL 1: BASIC SENTENCES

1. The **ember-red leaves** of autumn burn slowly. **COLOUR**
2. The **huffing wind** was too lazy to scatter the leaves. **UNUSUAL WIND VERBS**
3. Clouds form like **puffy plates**. **METAPHORS FOR THE CLOUDS**
4. The **leaves are a-flame** in a quilt of colour. **ARCHAIC WORDS FOR AUTUMN**

5. We enjoy **chomping** on blackcurrants. **AN AUTUMN FEAST**

6. The **fiery-reds** cast a rich hue on the forest. **COLOURS USING HEAT**

7. The **ghost-grey skies** of autumn change the mood. **OTHER IMAGES FOR AUTUMN**

8. Autumn is a time to be **afraid**. **SENSATION**

9. **A larder of aromas** drizzled from the trees. **SMELL**

10. The wild berries had **a savoury taste**. **TASTE**

LEVEL 2: A BASIC PARAGRAPH

The **leaves were molten-red**. The **yawning wind** made them shiver slightly. **Fluffy fleeces of cloud** passed over the forest. The **trees were a-flicker** like night lights. A group of children were **gulping** on wild gooseberries. The **blazing-brown** dome of leaves gave off a nice glow. **Owls haunted** and hunted through moon-splashed trees. We were **spooked** by their swivelling heads and lamp round eyes. **A perfumery of scents** hazed through the forest. The **ravishing taste** of freshly baked bread stayed in our memories.

LEVEL 3: CREATIVE PARAGRAPHS

The **barbecue-red leaves** hang silently on the trees. **Muffling winds** deaden all sound in the forest and slow the **billowy bells of cloud**. The oak **leaves are still a-light**, but barely. Dainty noses, sniffling and snuffling, glow the same mercury-red as the trees. They replace the sound of children **slobbering** over elderberries.

Fog-tinted fairy trees stand alone in fields, noosed by coils of dragon breath. A weak pitter-patter is heard, but it is not the sound of children's feet. It is the centuries-old, hissing drip of raindrops in caves. Spiders flood the forest, clutching their snare strings tightly, their eyes a-glitter with hatred. Owl-light replaces daylight as autumn comes to a close. The seething energy of the forest becomes vow-silent as promises to nature are kept. The burnt-red leaves turn a **smouldering-gold** as the first of the heavy rains fall.

The **rain drenches** everyone. They are not the soft, sodden, swollen raindrops of summer. They are not the light, aerated mizzling of spring showers. They are plump, pregnant with moisture, ploppy and destructive. The long, straight streaks of cloud we call mare's tails do not carry them. The skies are damnation-black and churning with anger. There is a cataclysm coming. It is time for **daunting** winter to display his wares.

The **hotchpotch of aromas** that graced the air is gone. The **delectable, marchpane** taste of the autumn harvest has faded from the palate. When the first snowfall comes, the world will be mummified in a powdery silence. It is time to be afraid again.

LEVEL 4: COMPLEX SENTENCES

Autumn is alien. The season of bumper harvests and swaying hay is soon replaced by Hallowe'en and horror. It is a portal to a time of dread, when winter's suffocating skies throttle the land. At its most glorious, autumn is spectacular. The world is a-blaze in its fiery cloak of colours, from incandescent-red to lightning-gold. Then both leaf-flame and field-light burn bright one last time, 'ere fading into the dying embers of their memory. The pyrotechnic show is over. The lifeless smell of monotoned winter invades the air.

Autumn starts with edibles exploding from the crackly mattress of the floor. Above them, the leaves become **conflagration-red**. It is the signal for ripened berries to fall from weary bushes. They make a phut-phut-phut sound as they hit the ground. Bronzed nuts, unhinged by **the wheezing wind**, go thunk-thunk-thunk as they fall like scattered gunshot.

The forest becomes an Abraham's bosom for a few brief months. As the nights turn chill, the urge for food is rekindled. The sound of animals **masticating** on nuts and slurping on berries fills the forest one last time. Then they delve, dig and disappear in order to escape the coming onslaught. Clouds fill up the sky like **vaporous veils**, intent on causing mischief. The canopy of the trees is still **a-smoulder**, but it won't last long. The **sweltering-oranges**, riot-reds and burning-yellows will soon fade. The waxing moon and the waning sun vie for supremacy. The sun, Gods daystar, is as luminous as his left eye. The moon, his night star, is as phosphorescent as his right.

Eventually, the moon wins the timeless battle of the ages. The molten-gold sheets of summer light turn into despairing fingers of moonlight. They poke through the trees rather than drown the forest's floor. **The straining light of the autumn moon** creates a dome of soft glow above the trees. This lends an eerie glamour to their death sleep. The wind dies with the tree-fire on occasion, creating a terrible silence. There is no insect-hum, no leaf-rustle, no wind-music. The winged symphony of birdsong no longer rings out. In the rivers, the spawning salmon starve and die. The last dragonfly whirrups and flutters, his wings a-glirr in that magical space between river and mist. He too must die. It is the tragedy and the glory of the cycle of life.

Hallowe'en creeps up with sinister intent. Scallions still grow in the forest, but rapscallions come out at night. Jack-o'- lanterns leer at passers-by like fiery poltergeists. Visions of bogeymen and doom-witches steal into dreams. Accursed sounds lacerate the night sky and strange shapes enter the realm of the forest. Creaking trees become wailing banshees and screeching ghouls spill out of windy bottles. Phantom-eyed owls hoot and haunt the night, ghosting through moon-stained trees. Deadly nightshade, lethal larkspur and poison hemlock burgle through the forest's floor. There's sorcery afoot, an alien and arcane hex that prowls and poisons the land. It is easy to become **unmanned** by it all. The mackerel skies of autumn, fringed with halogen-green and laced with lagoon-blue, give way to the claustrophobic skies of winter.

The **smorgasbords of scents** that have whirled around the forest are all gone. The **toothsome treats** of autumn are locked up in larders so mankind can survive the winter. Sly shadows return to the land. Wizened faces peep nervously from condensation-veiled windows. Doors are locked, kettles hiss, and fires splutter and cackle in cold grates once more. Parchment-faded faces puff on their pipes and mutter about the coldest winter in aeons approaching. The fading sunlight gasps its last, moulded-gold breath and turns pale until the first daffodils bloom again.

All living things seem to shrink into themselves, shrivelling and withering. There is a Reckoning coming of Dante-esque proportions. Winter's frigid fist is clenching and the last dragonfly seems but a flitting memory…

LEVEL 5: COMPLEX SENTENCES: THE END IS NIGH

A swirl of mist, a whirl of snow, a robe of shadow. It is the last day of autumn. The sere and yellow leaf is crumbling. A lesion of black light is churning in the sky. It bulges and swells, like a cauldron of doomsday-black. When it clears, it leaves a moon as bright and vile as the drop from a blood oath. Under a starless sky, Investigator Corbie, the king's monster hunter, is quarrying after the flesh-eaters. He has been hunting them for a long time.

When he started out on his quest, the rivers were kingfisher-blue and trickling. Now they are brandy-brown and make the land tremble. Instead of sowing fertility, they wreak havoc as they rumble and thunder through hidden valleys. Over the water, swirls of creamy mist steam in their own malice, as foul as any witches' soup.

The mountain range has been purged of its pristine-white majesty. It is unwelcoming and hazardous, draped in a fog of direness. Goblin-shrieks and wolf-howls carry down on the wind. It is a cold house for a monster hunter.

He has passed beaches where the sea buckles and creaks to the mercy of the heaving tide. The earthshine-gold aurora of summer has faded, leaving a storm-tossed seascape and a tempest of wind. He saw the sea stewing in its bruised-blue hatred and wisely took the route overland. He left it to carve its age-old carnage into the cliffs.

He saw the sensuous and sylph-like waterfalls of yore turn in to raging harridans. Now they are bullwhip-brown and lash the naked rock instead of caressing it. Neither are they inlaid with silver seams. Their brows are knitted with rage and edged with anger.

Whirls of snow ghost down over the forest. He was there to reap the early harvest of its nut-brown goodness. No more does it provide a culinary bounty for men of the bow; horsetails of moss hang like a spectre's entrails, the boughs are like the despairing limbs of the damned and only pools of shadow haunt the open spaces. It is abandoned and forlorn.

Sinews of fey-grey fog writhe over the pulsing lakes. The rain falls like the devil's spit, hot and hissing. No longer becalmed and glassy, they have a hazy, phantasmal aspect to them. Boiling with the incessant rain, they slowly swell in the bosom of the valley.

A tremulous purring begins in the sky above him. It's a barely suppressed rage, a growling from the gods. The carnal-black clouds begin to coalesce together like immense raven wings. A great clanking is heard. It is akin to some massive body of metal being dragged against its will across the sky. Heaven's forge gives out a last clanging gong, its final warning. It resonates and reverberates in a concussion of sound, a deafening convocation of hatred. The world falls crypt-still, waiting for the jarring collision of hot and cold air. The clouds converge into one mass, like a vast shield of vaporous hatred. It seems to steam like ichor, the black blood of the gods. There's a bellow, then a boom like a volcano erupting.

A great scar of seething light appears in the clouds' centre. The sound of humming, like a straining dam, trembles in the air. The lacerations of light seem to whine as great forks of flame-gold burst forth. Wriggling and writhing, they branch out like a wizard's whip. They zigzag through the agonized air, blazing like crippled capillaries. The lightning flashes once more, illuminating itself like the crawling cracks on stained glass. Then it sizzles itself to silence, its searing stilled, its anger quieted.

He has seen the bedewed spring and the bedizened summer come and go. He has hunted blood-besmeared trolls and dread vampyres. He longs for home but he must forge ahead. He is so close. He drops the human thigh bone back in to the midden heap. He doesn't have the words to describe the horror he feels. He needs help with that. In two days, he will catch them. The last three leaves of autumn are splashed on the trees like an afterthought in the easel of the gods. With the rumour of his passing, they slowly twirl to the ground, Van Gogh-red and tragic. Autumn is over.

He steps into the penumbra of shadow between two trees and into the next chapter of his life, waiting for the diction of horror to arrive with the cannibals.

ASSONANCE

Assonance occurs when the same, or similar, vowel sounds are used in two or more words in a passage of writing. Assonance has the power to dictate the mood of a passage. It can make it seem lonely or joyful and it can make it sad or uplifting. There are five vowels which can potentially affect the mood of a passage: **'a', 'e', 'i', 'o' and 'u'**.

Using the letters **'e'** and **'i'** in a group of words usually signifies that the passage will be light hearted or neutral of tone. By using a deliberate concentration of joyful words associated with these vowels, it can change the tone of a passage. Examples are given in the grid below.

The letter **'u'** is very neutral. It can be used in a lot of words without any noteworthy effect on a passage. It can be combined with 'o' to make a very effective combination, however. An example of this is words that end in 'ous': tremendous, wondrous and marvellous, for example. This then gives a passage an injection of energy and dynamism.

The letter **'a'** is also neutral as a general rule. It can be used for evoking scenes with water if it used properly by including an 's' at the end of the word.. In particular, it can be very effective if you wish to conjure up the sounds of splashing through a bog or sitting by a river.

The most common and effective use of assonance is the use of the **'o'** sound. This imbues the passage with sadness and evokes pathos in a reader. "The wind moaned through the cold house of the old man". Although the vowel sounds are not perfectly pitched, it is still effective. These half-sounds (through and house) are still very effective in conveying the loneliness of the house. That is because they are long vowel sounds and they add an air of gloom to the mood.

SAD 'O' SOUNDS	**JOYFUL 'I' SOUNDS**	**WET 'A' SOUNDS**
woe	Zion	sprays
lonely	smile	plashes
morose	blithe	swales
sorrow	divine	saturates
sombre	delight	splashes
forlorn	paradise	bathes
doleful	sunshine	paddles
mournful	satisfied	pampas grasses
desolate	sprightly	laves
lachrymose	light hearted	quagmires

WINTER

SNOW COLOUR

LEVEL 1	LEVEL 2	LEVEL 3	LEVEL 4	LEVEL 5	OTHERS
bleach-white	arctic-white	vampire-white	quicklime-white	whey-white	
whalebone-white	polar-white	zombie-white	skull-white	crystalline-white	

1. The bleach-white snow didn't stop *whiskey-nosed Santa* from coming.
2. The arctic-white snow didn't delay *chipmunk-cheeked Santa* one bit.
3. The vampire-white snow didn't halt the passage of *swag-bellied Santa*.
4. The quicklime-white snow didn't impede the progress of *cherub-cheeked Santa*.
5. The whey-white snow sky didn't make *Methuselah-bearded Santa* falter one jot.

SOUND

blasting storms	flogging squalls	lashing rainstorms	mangling winds	sundering cyclones	
battering gusts	flaying thunderstorms	lacerating hurricanes	razing windstorms	eviscerating tempests	

1. The storms were blasting outside as the fire inside *flooded my face with heat*.
2. The thunderstorms were flaying the trees outside as the fire *saturated my face with heat*.
3. The rainstorms were lashing the land outside as the fire *engulfed my face with heat*.
4. Razing windstorms scoured the land while the glowing fire *steeped the room in heat*.
5. Sundering cyclones buffeted the land as I let the fire's heat *immerse my face in warmth*.

STORMS USING PATHETIC FALLACY

screaming winds	shrieking winds	wailing winds	yowling winds	keening winds	
screeching	snarling	whining	mewling	caterwauling	

| winds | winds | winds | winds | winds | |

1. Screaming winds passed over the house as our Christmas **sparklers spat and fizzed**.
2. Snarling winds raged outside as **wall shadows danced to the fire's flame**.
3. The wailing winds outside didn't stop our **window candles winking at the neighbours**.
4. The mewling winds couldn't stop our **magnesium-bright angel glittering atop the tree**.
5. The keening winds made the **blazing jig of the fire dance all the merrier**.

SILENCE

a quiet peace	a death-like silence	an awful shush	an alien serenity	an unearthly soundlessness	
a gentle hush	a tomb-like stillness	a terrible calmness	an eerie tranquillity	a shocking quiescence	

1. The **crackers popped and exploded** as a quiet peace cloaked the land outside.
2. A death-like silence draped the land as our **crackers snapped and burst**.
3. An awful shush garbed the shrouded the land as our **kettle hissed and whined**.
4. An eerie tranquillity sheathed the world outside as our **glasses clinked and pinged**.
5. A shocking quiescence garbed the world outside as our **champagne flutes tinkled and pinged**.

SKY COLOUR

grit-grey skies	flint-grey skies	lead-grey skies	shackle-grey skies	fetter-grey skies	
gravel-grey skies	cinder-grey skies	shale-grey skies	manacle-grey skies	fey-grey skies	

1. The grit-grey skies looked down as the **kettle bubbled and boiled**.
2. The cinder-grey skies gazed down as the **fire cackled and crackled**.
3. The lead-grey skies stared silently outside as the **fire's flames licked the hearth**.
4. The manacle-grey sky brooding outside didn't stop us **chortling and chuckling with joy**.
5. **Laughter was ringing and resonating** through the house, defying the fetter-grey sky outside.

BARREN SKIES

empty skies	bleak skies	haunting skies	wan skies	skeletal skies	
lonely skies	bitter skies	pasty skies	blanched skies	cadaverous skies	

1. The *fire baptised us in heat* as the lonely sky outside hung sadly.
2. The *fire felt like warm butter melting on our faces* as the bitter sky outside wept.
3. The *fire felt like a sunset glow on our faces* as the haunting skies remained melancholy.
4. The blanched skies looked lachrymose as the *fire's heat pulsed with waves of warmth* **like an oven**.
5. The cadaverous sky seemed lugubrious as the *fire's warmth washed over us like the wafts from a volcano vent*.

CHOKING WINTER

winter chokes	winter smothers	winter stifles	winter constricts	winter garrottes	
winter squeezes	winter strangles	winter suffocates	winter throttles	winter asphyxiates	

1. Winter choked the land as *a pale, winter's* **moon** hung in the sky.
2. Winter strangled the land as *a pearly moon* filled the sky.
3. The pitiless winter suffocated the land as *an opalescent moon* framed the sky.
4. The vengeful winter throttled the land as *the nacreous moon* seemed to flood the land with its pallid light.
4. The vindictive winter garrotted the land as *the phosphorescent brilliance of the moon* illuminated the sky.

SMELL

spicy beef	mulled wine	oaken oven smells	sulphurous crackers	frankincense-scented	

				candles	
peppery scents	malt liqueurs	exotic stove smells	the whiff of cordite from crackers	myrrh-scented candles	

1. The smell of spiced beef filled the room as *forks of flame* chased the shadows away.
2. The plummy scent of mulled wine filled the room as *feathers of flame* made the sparks sizzle.
3. Exotic stove smells flooded the room as *ribbons of flame* danced happily in the grate.
4. Sulphurous crackers snapped and burst as *quiffs of flame* made the sound of a billowing sheet.
5. Myrrh-scented candles flickered quietly as *tongues of flame* licked the hearth.

SENSATION

shivering bodies	stiff limbs	chattering teeth	skin-seeping cold	chilblained feet	
quivering bodies	sore joints	tingling fingertips	brandy-noses snuffle	hypothermia and gangrene	

1. Our bodies shivered as *the radiant light* of the fire warmed us up.
2. Our stiff limbs defrosted as *the lambent light* of the fire heated us up.
3. Our tingling fingertips stretched closer as *the fulgent light* of the fire gave us cheer.
4. Our brandy-noses snuffled as the *refulgent light* of the fire doused us with its light.
5. Our chilblained feet tingled and nipped as *the effulgent light* of the fire hypnotised us and turned us all into fire gazers.

TASTE

seasoned vegetables	tea tannins	sparkling champagne	gamy goose	fat-dripping duck	
buttery potatoes	mushroom vol-au-vents	yeasty beer	plummy puddings	thyme-filled turkeys	

1. The buttery potatoes went down well as the Christmas presents were *a-shine* in the corner.
2. The tea tannins felt wholesome as the Christmas ornaments were *a-dazzle* all around us.
3. The sparkling champagne tasted divine and the glasses were *a-glitter* from the fire.
4. The gamy goose was packed with herbs and spices. It steamed quietly as the decorations were *a-flash* all around the room.
5. The joy of Christmas seemed to have been poured into the thyme-filled turkey. It tasted heavenly as glasses clinked, laughter rang out and the candles were *a-flicker* with delight.

LEVEL 1: BASIC SENTENCES

1. The snow was **whalebone-white**. **SNOW COLOUR**
2. The **battering** gusts were awful. **SOUND**
3. The **screeching** winds were dreadful. **STORMS**
4. A **gentle hush** cloaked the land. **SILENCE**
5. The **gravel-grey** skies were bare. **SKY COLOUR**
6. The **empty** skies were silent. **BARREN SKIES**
7. Winter **squeezes** everything to death. **CHOKING WINTER**
8. **Peppery scents** filled the room. **SMELL**
9. Our **quivering bodies** were cold. **SENSATION**
10. The **seasoned** vegetables were delicious. **TASTE**

LEVEL 2: A BASIC PARAGRAPH

The snow was **polar-white**. The **flogging squalls** of winter blew loudly. **Screeching winds** occasionally rose up. When they died, a **tomb-like silence** haunted the land. **Flint-grey skies** oversaw the land. The **bleak skies** were depressing. Winter **smothered the land** with its vice-like grip. **Malt liqueurs**, taken to warm up chilled bodies, were a poor substitute for the sun. **Sore joints** creaked and groaned like rusty hinges. The scent of **creamy, mushroom vol-au-vents** floating through the house cheered us up.

LEVEL 3: CREATIVE PARAGRAPHS

The snow was **zombie-white**. Winter's **lacerating hurricanes** and **whining winds** had come and gone, leaving a **terrible calmness**. The skies above were an unholy mixture of **shale-grey** clouds and **pasty** streaks. Callous winter was **stifling** the world with its icy breath. I could see a group of kidults playing on a frozen pond. They stamped their frozen feet and thumped their chilly bodies to warm up. Their ears caught fire and turned an icy-blue where their scarves couldn't reach. Nose-icicles dripped from their frozen faces. Their wheezy, wind-filled lungs were belching out steam as they itched and scratched at their raw skin. They started skating. They slipped, slid and slithered on the polished ice. Hissing and swishing with their skates, they swooped and whooped across the ice. Then they screamed as the ice broke. It must have felt like lances of fire lighting up their skin as they fell in to the perishing cold water.

Their teeth were chattering when they crawled back out. They followed the **oaken oven smells** home to warm up. I hoped that the **yeasty beer** would warm their hearts as their bodies were frozen.

LEVEL 4: ADVANCED PARAGRAPHS

I stared into the fire. It crackled and spat before hissing into life. Its lambent light stole away the velvet-black shadows dancing on the wall. Flames of rainbow-orange licked hungrily at the chimney as they clambered as higher and higher. The fire's hypnotic jig of joy was as much a celebration as ours. It wanted to be alive on Christmas Day also. A pageant of smells filled the house. Thyme-filled turkeys sizzled on the oven foil. They battled to take over from the lavender-scented candles and the sulfurous smell of crackers. I could hear them snapping and exploding in another room. The scrumptious smell of goose grease wafted into the room, sifting out the other smells. The children had been up early, hoping that the greatest illusionist of them all had visited.

Swag-bellied Santa used sleigh-in-hand rather than sleight-of-hand, but his brand of escapism beat Houdini every time. This jolly, whiskey-nosed character has conjured up more delight from souls than the rest of humanity combined. His marmot-cheeked magic is indeed a joy to the world. I heard the welcome sound of the kettle boiling. It was bubbling and hissing in the background. Warmth flooded the room as the fire came alive. The sound of chuckling and chortling floated to my ears. The Christmas tree flashed and flickered with its dazzling lights. An angel was perched on the top, glittering with its flash-silver lustre. A single candle twinkled merrily in the window. The jingling of the dinner bell rang. It's the greatest sound that winter could offer. I sighed with happiness and followed the smells and laughter to my chair.

LEVEL 5: COMPLEX WRITING: WINTER WONDERLAND

My boots crunched through the powdered snow. They detonated like Christmas crackers every time my feet hit the ground. The world around me was imprisoned in a glair-white silence. Nothing sounded, nothing stirred, nothing sang. Winters slavering fangs had come and gone. Its lacerating winds had stripped the last leaves from the trees, leaving them naked and brooding in a harsh world. They were wrapped in their surgical coats now, groaning under the weight of the snow. Occasionally, a great limb would creak, crack and collapse. It sounded like an explosion going through the forest. Other than that, an alien serenity garbed the forest. There was no dawn chorus, no symphony of sound, no avian orchestra. The world was entombed in a dome of silence. Winter's deadly clutch had strangled and stifled all life from the land.

A week ago, a great storm had come screeching through. It had snarled and mewled with its deadly voice, sounding like a wailing spectre. It had ripped slates from roofs and its slavering fangs had sent the last of the squirrels into hibernation. Its scavenging skies had compressed down upon the land, surveying it with a deadly malice. The rain it had brought with it was bitter, like ice-silver bullets of spite. It had gashed and gouged at every living thing, sparing no one. Doom-laden clouds, bloated with hatred, had roiled in the sky before unleashing their vengeful wares. Now the blaring of the wind and blasting of the rain was over. This was the aftershock. The world was becalmed. The furious winter tempests had given too much of themselves. They were spent.

High above me, the last of the morning stars were winking out sadly. They flashed their last, like bling-silver grains of sand in the dawn sky. Their bejewelled brilliance fading into nothingness was a wonder to behold. A ghostly, orb-white, winter moon hung there, imitating a pale strobe light. A corona of shimmering yellow ringed its dying glory. The sky around it was a wide sheet of grate-grey, hemmed in the horizon with a plum-purple tinge. It was a snow sky, Gods perfect gift for Christmas. Fluttery snowflakes puffed down on me, sylph-like in their airy silence. They created a mantle of Lapland-white. When they landed, they glinted like pulverized diamond dust. It was as if I was walking through an outdoor version of the mines of Solomon, a sparkling winterscape of white and silver.

Far below me, coils of smoke drifted up from sleepy hamlets. The cocoon of silence was ruptured by the sound of squealing. Some children were up early, playing on the duck-pond. From my height, it looked like a frozen salver of polished glass. The zero temperatures had encased the water in a prison of silver. In the distance, the peaks of the mountains were wreathed in a necklace of snow. The sun was coming up behind one of them, looking like a glowing torc as its full majesty was blocked by the mountains enormity. It threw down its watery shards of sunlight in vain. Its power was muted by nature's iron-clad laws. Nothing it could do could banish the wonderland of white beneath it. Its only effect was to smash the flint-grey sky into wonderful striations of yellow, pink and orange. It was enough. The ornamental beauty of the land returned. All around me, the snow flashed and glittered like angel-fire. As my walk ended, I marvelled at the might of nature. Its awe inspiring majesty made my soul rejoice.

REPETITION

Repetition occurs when a word, phrase or sentence is deliberately used more than once for dramatic effect. Its primary function is to reinforce an idea or mood for the reader. For example, a student could plan to open his essay with a phrase that is repeated. "It was **so cold**. It was **so cold** that the lake froze over". The danger here is that a corrector might think that his/her vocabulary was limited. There are a range of other words like algid, gelid and frigid that could have been used. As such, it may be wiser to encourage its use among more advanced students.

If repetition is to be used, it might be best to link the 'hook sentence' (the opening sentence) to the 'unhook sentence' (the closing sentence). For example, in the level 5 essay in the spring section, I employed that technique deliberately. The first line states: "Spring is **glee**". That is the hook sentence. The unhook sentence was linked by one word to the hook sentence: "If it were a perfume, it would be called eau-de-**Glee**". The theme throughout the essay concerned the joy and glee of spring. It is important that a hook sentence and an unhook sentence should be consistent with the theme of the passage in mind.

Elsewhere in the book, there aren't too many examples of repetition. In the mountain chapter, level 5, I did shorten the sentences and used repetition for dramatic effect. "**All** was silent. **All** was still". It adds to the dramatic effect when repetition is used in this fashion. The fluidity of the writing grinds to a juddering halt through the short sentences.

The paragraphs, essays and chapters all have a common repetitive element. In each case, I finished them with the senses of smell and taste. That is because the nose contains 1,000 smell receptors and it can identify or distinguish between approximately 10,000 different scents. Similarly, the mouth, lips, tongue and roof of the mouth contain roughly 1,000 taste buds also. It is interesting that we can only recognize four main tastes: sweet, sour, salty and bitter. If we were to block our nose while eating, that is the extent of our tastes! It is the *smell* of food rather than the taste that tells us what is scrumptious and what is not.

We are bombarded by a stew of smells and tastes every day. Most of the time it is a subliminal experience. It is registered in the back of our mind, our subconscious, but not our conscious mind. I set out to leave the smell and taste of food and drink lingering in a tantalizing way for the reader. By repeating it in every chapter, I was hoping to reinforce the importance of the 'neglected' senses of smell and taste. If your students can include it in their writing, they will give themselves and the reader a more visceral experience.

MONSTERS

ANIMAL EYES

LEVEL 1	LEVEL 2	LEVEL 3	LEVEL 4	LEVEL 5	OTHERS
feline/cat	lupine/wolf	vulpine/fox	simian/gorilla	anguine/snake	
serpentine/snake	leonine/lion	taurine/bull	saurian/lizard	arachnid/spider	

1. He had slitted, feline eyes and *cruel, curved eyebrows*.
2. He had feral, lupine eyes and *arched, brambly eyebrows*.
3. He had glinting, vulpine eyes and *sickle-shaped eyebrows*.
4. He had gleaming, saurian eyes and *scythe-shaped eyebrows*.
5. He had the glittering eyes of an arachnid and his *eyebrows were shaped like slash-hooks*.

EVIL EYES

blazing with anger	flashing with cruelty	glinting with violence	simmering with spite	scorching with odium
flaming with hatred	gleaming with cunning	glittering with hostility	shining with malice	smouldering with vengeance

1. His eyes were *bloodshot* and blazed with anger.
2. He was *bug-eyed* and they flashed with cruelty.
3. His eyes were *blood-flecked* and glinted with violence.
4. He was *squint-eyed* and they simmered with spite.
5. He had a *basilisk's eyes* and they were smouldering with vengeance.

COLD EYES

frosty eyes	chilling eyes	Cossack-cold eyes	tundra-cold eyes	algid eyes	
wintry eyes	glacial eyes	cadaver-cold eyes	frigid eyes	gelid eyes	

1. His eyes were frosty, *two lifeless pools of abyss-black*.

2. He had chilling eyes, *two pitiless pools of pagan-black*.

3. He had cadaver-cold eyes, *two soulless pools of void-black*.

4. He had frigid eyes, *two merciless pools of cauldron-black*.

5. His eyes were as algid as an arctic wind, *two passionless pools of executioner-black*.

A HEARTLESS VOICE

a grave	a vault	a burial chamber	a sepulchre	an ossuary	
a tomb	a crypt	a barrow	a sarcophagus	a mausoleum	

1. His voice was as lonely as a grave and his *eyes were a soul-piercing, Hades-black*.

2. His voice was as friendless as a crypt and his *eyes were a soul-penetrating, Charon-black*.

3. His voice was as haunting as a barrow and his *eyes were a soul-scalding, Styx-black*.

4. His voice was as desolate as a sarcophagus and his *eyes were a soul-shrinking, Lethe-black*.

5. His voice was as devoid of life as an ossuary and his *eyes were a soul-withering, Acheron-black*.

SNAKY VOICE

an oily voice	a slick voice	fork-tongued	a wheedling voice	ingratiating voice	
a greasy voice	a fawning voice	honey-tongued	a toadying voice	a snake-oil salesman's	

1. He had an oily voice and *a crocodile's eyes*.

2. He had a slick voice and *the wild-eyed stare of a piranha*.

3. He was fork-tongued and had *the ice-cold eyes of a barracuda*.

4. He had a toadying voice and *the cobra-cold, bulbous eyes of an ogre*.

5. He had a snake-oil salesman's voice and *the hollowed, sunken eyes of a nightwalker*.

OTHER FEATURES

| thin, | jug ears | hatchet hard | pop eyes and | a devil's | |

| bloodless lips | | hands | a saucy beard | heart | |
| razor-thin lips | tankard handle ears | callused, knotty fingers | frenzied eyes and spittle-flecked lips | a fallow soul | |

1. His voice was hissing through his **broken-glass teeth** and thin, bloodless lips.

2. He had a gravelly voice, jug ears, and **teeth as cruel as talon tips**.

3. He had a jeering voice, hatchet hard hands, and his **teeth were filed down into harpoon tips**.

4. He had a wheezy voice, frenzied eyes with spittle-flecked lips, and he was as **snaggle-toothed as a witch**.

5. He had a cruel, stony voice, a fallow soul, and his **teeth were as jagged as shards of glass**.

NOSE

| a hawkish nose | vulturous | cob-nosed | pug-nosed | a raven's nose, hooked and cruel | |
| hook-nosed | barbarous | bulbous | snub-nosed | a witch's, crooked nose | |

1. He was hook-nosed and had **corpse-white skin**.

2. He had a barbarous nose and **paste-white skin**.

3. He was cob-nosed and his **skin was a shining, skull-white**.

4. He was snub-nosed and his **skin had an unhealthy, vampire-white glow**.

5. He had a raven's nose, hooked and cruel. His **skin had a zombie-white, lifeless sheen**.

HAIR

| lifeless hair | greasy hair | matted hair | lice-infected | pestilent | |
| lank hair | grimy hair | knotted hair | lustreless | oleaginous | |

1. He had lifeless hair and **dogtooth-yellow fangs**.

2. He had greasy hair and **leprous-yellow teeth**.

3. He had matted hair and **nicotine-yellow teeth**.

4. His hair was lustreless and his *teeth were a filthy, jaundice-yellow*.

5. His hair was diseased and pestilent and he had *septic, canker-yellow teeth*.

MOCKING GRINS

a smirk	a sly look	a leer	a lopsided grin	a condescending grin	
a sneer	a scornful look	a taunting look	a goblin grin	a sardonic smile	

1. He sneered at me and I could see his *fin-shaped fangs*.

2. He gave me a sly look and I could see his *saw-toothed incisors*.

3. His gaunt face gave me a taunting look and I could see his *twisted, scalpel-sharp canines*.

4. His pinched face flashed me a goblin grin and I backed away from his *serrated, shark's teeth*.

5. He was hatchet-faced with a condescending smile and I recoiled from his *crenelated, tombstone teeth*.

STRENGTH

a bull's neck	a caveman's shoulders	demonic power	Samson's strength	Neanderthal muscles	
a buffalo's neck	a gorilla's shoulders	a Titan's power	Goliath's strength	a troglodyte's muscles	

1. He had a bull's neck and *skin as rough as tree bark*.

2. He had a gorilla's shoulders and *skin as coarse as sandpaper*.

3. He had a Titan's power and his *face was as riffled as snakeskin leather*.

4. He had Samson's strength and *pockmarked, pitted skin*.

5. He had a brutish nose, Neanderthal muscles and an *alligator's skin, ridged and scaly*.

LEVEL 1: BASIC SENTENCES

1. He had **serpentine** eyes. **ANIMAL EYES**

2. They were **flaming with hatred**. **EVIL EYES**

3. He had **wintry** eyes. **COLD EYES**

4. His voice was **as lonely as a tomb**. **HEARTLESS VOICE**

5. He had a **greasy** voice. **SNAKY VOICE**

6. He had **razor-thin lips**. **OTHER FEATURES**

7. He had a **hawkish** nose. **NOSE**

8. He had **lank** hair. **HAIR**

9. He **smirked** at me. **MOCKING GRINS**

10. He had a **buffalo's** neck. **STRENGTH**

LEVEL 2: A BASIC PARAGRAPH

The monster looking at me had **leonine eyes**. They were **gleaming with cunning**. His pair of **glacial eyes** stared at me coldly. He voice was **as empty of life as a crypt**. He spoke in a **fawning** manner, trying to lure me into his lair. His **tankard handle ears** were enormous. They matched his **vulturous** nose. **Grimy hair** plastered his fierce face. He gave me a **scornful look** when I took a step back. His **caveman's shoulders** flexed once before he charged at me.

LEVEL 3: CREATIVE PARAGRAPHS

His **taurine** eyes were **glittering with hostility**. They were as wild and fearsome as any bull. He swung his mace and nearly decapitated me. I could feel its passage whisking my hair as I ducked. They were demons, these adversaries of ours. They hated the grain-eaters, or so they called us. They preferred to rip and gorge on human flesh and we were afraid of them. Some of them were hard of eye and stony of face. Others were wild-eyed savages with a berserk nature.

They all shared the same **Cossack-cold** look in their eyes. Their voices were **as lifeless as a burial chamber**. Even when they taunted us, when they tried to be **honey-tongued**, their voices echoed with brutality. Their **callused, knotty fingers** beckoned us to fight them and they smashed their fists against their **bulbous noses** to prove their bravery. Hairs as hard as a boar's bristles sprouted from their faces. Their head hair was **knotted** and clotted with dry, human blood. Cauliflower ears sprouted out from either side of the head, puffy and raw from countless battles. Even their faces were bestial, nicked and notched from axe and sword.

He gave me a **leer** as he swung his mace with that **demonic** power of his. Battle fever rose up in me and I blocked him. I was determined to spill his blood before he did it to me.

LEVEL 4: ADVANCED PARAGRAPHS

The battle had not gone as we had planned. Pockets of our men still fought for their lives, but it was looking grim for us. Our opponents were too strong, too fast and too deadly. I stared at the man trying to kill me. He had the **simian eyes of an ape, crafty and cunning.** They **were simmering with spite** as I raised a tired sword arm to defend myself.

They seemed **tundra-cold** and merciless, two pools of chilling, **cauldron-black.** I was disturbed when he laughed at my weakness. He beckoned me to attack him and spoke with a strange, guttural accent. His attempt at a **wheedling voice** was laughable. It was cold and **echoed like a deep sepulchre.** There was a gravelly aspect to it, as if stones were scraping together. His voice fitted his **pop eyes and saucy beard** perfectly. It seemed like he had fangs instead of teeth because they were shaped like broken stalagmites.

Hanks of his **lice-infected hair** lay plastered over a **pug nose**, crooked and dented. He had a pair of hirsute and crescent-shaped eyebrows. They stood out because his skin was as pale as a winter's moon. It was smooth and greasy, one of the hallmarks of a cannibal. I whacked the pommel of my sword off his **granite jaw**, but it had no effect.

He cast me a **lopsided grin** and I realized then that he had **Goliath's strength.** I knew I wouldn't survive for much longer. I was bone tired and battle drunk. It was almost a relief when he raised his cudgel for the final strike. I closed my weary eyes and waited.

LEVEL 5: COMPLEX WRITING: THE BATTLE

The arrows whizzed over our heads. They glinted and fizzed, their shafts causing the air around them to sizzle. They were like little pins of hissing silver under the doom-laden sky, whistling their way gleefully towards their targets. The clouds above them were Barabbas-black and churning. I looked at the army we faced and the thought struck me that we would not survive the day.

Our enemies were more beast than man. Their **arachnid eyes** were pitiless and **as gelid as a mausoleum.** They were **scorching with odium** under their **oleaginous hair.** Their hair hung over their **witches', crooked noses.** A **troglodyte's muscles** lay within those ox-yoke shoulders. Fountains of volcano-red blood would vent into the air when their pulverizing weapons hit the target. They carried maces, pikes, shillelaghs and bludgeons; weapons designed to smash, club, pound and shatter.

Our thin, zinc-silver armour was no match for their brutality. It gleamed like moon flame and was just as fragile. The sound of bones snapping and cracking rent the air. It competed with the screams of the dying and the curses of the living. The lucky ones died quickly. Their last sight would not be a set of scalpel-sharp incisors straining downwards to rip their soft flesh. Our foe had the **cruel hearts** of a nest of devils.

I hated them for their corpse-white skin. It was as scaly as an alligators, ridged and tough. I hated them for their **galling, sardonic grins** and their **ingratiating voices**. They were constantly calling out in a tongue alien to ours. Most of all, I hated them for their eyes. They all carried the same look, two soul-withering pools of Acheron-black. Boiling with fervour, all the hatred of a thousand years was festering in them.

At my feet, the battle field was anointed with the blood of the fallen. It was glossy and slick, a slippery web of entrails and bowels. Fire arrows fell all around me, frizzling and spitting when they scorched into the blood. A huge beast with a singed face appeared in front of me. His eyebrows were fire worshipper-black and scythe-shaped. He clanked his huge mace into my helmet and the world went dark…

*Type '**Describing a Zombie**' and '**Describing a Witch**' into Google to see further examples of this genre. They are both to be found under the '**Best Descriptive Writing**' heading.

TRIPLICATION

Triplication occurs when words or phrases are repeated in groups of three. It is a highly impactful device when used in a constructive manner. Although technically it is the threefold repetition of a word or phrase, there is a case for arguing that grouping nouns, verbs or adjectives in sequences of three qualifies it to be called triplication. The desert chapter has examples of both.

"We were flamed and fried in the desert heat. It seemed to hate **everything that** walked, **everything that** crawled and **everything that** flew". This is a very obvious example of triplication as the words "everything that" are repeated thrice. It is less clear if using three nouns followed by verbs for each one qualifies, but I would argue that it does. In the desert chapter, a sentence using that formula is used. "Your **blood simmers**, your **brain stews** and even your **bones smoulder**". The sentence is alliterative also and it is a mnemonic sentence as a result. There is a rhythm and a balance provided to the sentence that is conveyed by the arrangement of the words.

Triplication can also be used to make a scene seem dramatic or to pause the movement of the action. In the mountain section, Level 4, triplication was employed to evoke the sense of emptiness and loneliness at the roof of the world. "**Nothing** stirred. **Nothing** sounded. **Nothing** sang". Its purpose in this case was to leave the reader with a sense of the desolation of a mountain. By mirroring and repeating the word "nothing", it reinforces the concept of nothingness and solitude. In this way, the mood of the passage is affected.

Some of the world's greatest writers have used the idea of objects and events occurring in threes. Shakespeare, Tolkien, the Grimm brothers and Chaucer were particularly dependent on events taking place in groups of three. Many of our most ancient folk tales and heroic stories have their genesis in this basic concept. Whether it is a genie granting three wishes or three bears in a cabin, they remain the enduring legacy of earlier folk myths.

Getting a student to use verbs in groups of three is a great way to provide a punch in their story. It can change the narrative style to dramatic effect and may even provide a musical resonance within the story. A simple sentence using three verbs can capture the manic energy of a sports stadium. "The crowd were a **chanting, cackling, cantankerous** bunch". "The stadium was a **throbbing, trembling, threshing** army of bodies". Both of these sentences, although not examples of triplication, are good examples of how to encourage its use in the long term.

Writing with Stardust

THE DESERT

COLOUR

LEVEL 1	LEVEL 2	LEVEL 3	LEVEL 4	LEVEL 5	OTHERS
barren-brown	scorched-brown	fallow-brown	wasteland-brown	burnt-umber	
blasted-brown	singed-brown	fuscous-brown	wind-scoured brown	burnt-sienna	

1. The blasted-brown desert was **an arena of death**.
2. The scorched-brown desert was **a theatre of death**.
3. The fallow-brown desert was **a coliseum of death**.
4. The wasteland-brown desert was **a monstrous amphitheatre of death**.
5. The burnt-umber desert was **a vast, scorching pan of emptiness**.

SOUND

sneaking	scrambling	scratching	slithering	sidling	
scraping	scrawling	scrabbling	slinking	skulking	

1. The scraping sounds of animals at night **drove us mad**.
2. The scrambling sounds of animals beyond the campfire **unmanned us**.
3. The scratching sounds of animals beyond the firelight **unhinged us**.
4. The slithering sounds of snakes outside of the fire's glow **drove us demented**.
5. The skulking of animals stalking us at night **tipped us over the edge and into insanity**.

INACTION

empty	arid	desiccated	featureless	sterile	
lifeless	barren	desolate	forlorn	jejune	

1. We were **gasping for breath** through the lifeless desert.
2. Our **breath was puffing** in the arid desert.
3. Our **lungs were huffing** through the desiccated desert.

4. Our burnt **lungs were chugging** through the forlorn desert.

5. Our singed **lungs were wheezing and pumping** like a bellows through the jejune desert.

METAPHORS

the devil's kitchen	Satan's sauna	Lucifer's garden	the devil's cauldron	Abaddon's arboretum	
Old Nick's oven	Satan's solarium	Lucifer's grill	the devil's crematorium	Beelzebub's bake house	

1. The desert by day is the devil's kitchen. The nights are *as cold as a witch's soul*.

2. The desert by day is Satan's sauna. The nights are *as cold as a phantom's soul*.

3. The desert by day is Lucifer's garden. The nights are *as cold as the devil's soul*.

4. The desert by day is the devil's cauldron. The desert by night is *as cold as a banshee's soul*.

5. The desert by day is Beelzebub's bake house. The desert by night is *as cold as a ghoul's soul*.

ANIMALS OF THE DESERT

camel	desert lion	desert fox	scorpion	tarantula	
lizard	bobcat	coyote	rattlesnake	vampire bat	

1. Camels can live in deserts *as hot as a furnace*.

2. Bobcats can survive in deserts *as hot as a lime kiln*.

3. Coyotes can inhabit stifling deserts *as hot as Greek fire*.

4. Scorpions dwell in suffocating deserts *as hot as a dragon's breath*.

5. Tarantulas thrive in perfidious deserts *as hot as the devil's breath*.

PLANTS OF THE DESERT

cactus	brittle bush	jumping cholla	pancake cactus	desert ironwood	
soap tree	chain fruit	ocotillo	creosote bush	Joshua tree	

1. The cactus was circled by *a shimmering heat haze*.

2. The chain fruit was surrounded by *a dream-like mirage*.

3. The ocotillo was encircled by *a trance-like mirage*.

4. The creosote bush was enwreathed by a mirage. It was like *an illusory mirror of your own doom*.

5. The Joshua tree was begirded by a mirage. It looked to us like *a hallucinatory, graven image of our own death*.

BIRDS OF THE DESERT

crow	eagle	humming bird	cactus wren	roadrunner	
owl	hawk	desert quail	cactus woodpecker	vulture	

1. The *sun blazes*, the *heat bakes* and your *skin boils*.

2. The *sun scorches*, the *heat swelters* and only the *dust sparkles*.

3. The desert is *barren, bleak and bereft* of life.

4. Your *blood simmers*, your *brain stews* and even your *bones smoulder*.

5. The heat is *relentless, remorseless and reckless* in its hatred of every living thing.

SMELL

burned and blasted	baked and barbecued	griddled and grilled	scorched and seared	simmered and skewered	
flamed and fried	basted and blazed	roasted and sautéed	combusted and cooked	sizzled and toasted	

1. We were flamed and fried in the desert heat. It seemed to hate *everything that walked*, *everything that crawled* and *everything that flew*.

2. We were baked and barbecued in the desert heat. At night, the *temperatures plummet*, the *mercury dips* and even the *thermometers shiver*.

3. We were griddled and grilled by the desert sun. The days were *searing*, the sun was *scouring* and the sand was *singeing*.

4. We were scorched and seared by the desert sun. Walls of sand *flayed, flogged* and *flagellated* our skin.

5. We were sizzled and toasted by the remorseless sun. Even the nights were *starlit*, but *sinister*, not *soul-nourishing*.

SENSATION

a dry, gritty mouth	swollen tongue	parched throat	feet like hot coals	skin scraped by sandpaper	
sweat sodden	brain inflamed	dehydrated liver	face like Greek fire	skin stabbed by sun-spears	

1. Our mouths were dry and gritty. By day, there is no life in the desert: *no joy*, *no movement* and *no hope*.
2. Our brains seemed inflamed by the heat. The desert is *stark* and *sterile* and *savage*.
3. Our parched throats were not the problem. The desert vegetation ripped at us with *barb*, *hook* and *thorn*, like mini-armour ranged against us.
4. Our faces felt like Greek fire had been poured on them. Every creature that *scuttled*, *slithered* or *skittered* had burrowed underground long ago.
5. Vultures circled overhead like winged messengers of death as the sun stabbed us with its spears. We *trudged*, *tottered* and *tacked* inch by tortoise inch towards our inevitable death.

TASTE

joyless taste	juiceless taste	listless taste	vapid taste	mawkish taste	
tasteless	spiritless taste	savourless taste	insipid taste	wersh taste	

1. The *scalding* sun makes the food seem tasteless.
2. The *simmering* sun makes the food seem juiceless.
3. The *seething* sun makes the food appear savourless.
4. The *smouldering* sun turns the food insipid.
5. The *sweltering* sun renders the food wersh and mawkish.

LEVEL 1: BASIC SENTENCES

1. The desert was **barren-brown**. **COLOUR**

2. Little creatures were **sneaking** through the desert. **SOUND**

3. The desert was **empty** of life. **INACTION**

4. The desert is **Old Nick's oven**. **METAPHORS**

5. **Lizards** skittered across the golden sand. **ANIMALS**

6. **Soap trees** stared silently at the sun. **PLANTS**

7. **Crows** called out in their horrible voices. **BIRDS**

8. Everything smelled **burned and blasted**. **SMELL**

9. We were **sweat sodden** by the heat. **SENSATION**

10. The food tasted **joyless**. **TASTE**

LEVEL 2: A BASIC PARAGRAPH

The desert was **singed-brown**. **Scrawling sounds** filled the air at night time. The land was flat and **barren**. The nomad's called it **Satan's solarium**. Even the **desert lions** were more ferocious than is usual. Only the odd **brittle bush** broke up the emptiness of the desert. A screaming **hawk** flew overhead. Like us, it was being **basted and blazed** by the sun. Our **tongues were swollen** from the lack of water. Our food had a **spiritless taste** to it.

LEVEL 3: CREATIVE PARAGRAPHS

The **fuscous-brown** desert was killing me. I had seen neither man nor beast for three days and my water was gone. It was the most **desolate** and lonesome environment I had ever been in. I felt like a castaway on a sea of sand. The **scratching** sounds outside the light of the campfire last night were the only signs of life. **Lucifer's grill** itself could not have scorched away all the evidence of nature as this place had. I thought I saw the paw prints of a **desert fox** once, the wraith of the desert. Maybe it was just my insanity seeing at the cloven hoofs of the devil in the sand.

The monotony of this parched wilderness was difficult to explain. It was a crucible of death, a bone-dry basin of vastness and death. The immensity of it burned into your brain, your only visual relief being a spiny cactus or **jumping cholla** bush. As far as the eye could see, everything was being **roasted and sautéed** with the same intensity. Just then, I thought I saw a **humming bird** flitting into a cactus, but it was probably another hallucination. My **dehydrated liver** was shutting down. The **listless taste** of my last biscuit was a distant memory as I limped and trudged towards my death

LEVELS 4 AND 5: USING THE SENSES

The desert hates me. I've been here three days without water, food or fire. I'm getting steadily weaker and I fear the worst. Getting separated from your caravan is just about the worst thing you can do out here in the devil's garden. Deaths hungry maw seeks me everywhere. There's no respite from it. The heat might be addling my brain but I think the desert suffers from schizophrenia. By day, the heat is like standing in front of a fiery dragon and by night, the cold is like being suspended in a cryogenics chamber. It's full and spiteful wrath bears down upon you constantly. It's a bi-polar paradox of heat and cold. There is no respite and no mercy.

The cancerous sun, the cankerous heat and the cantankerous cold are heart-haunting. Everything in this God-forsaken place is either wicked and warped or blasted and burned. Who ever heard of an environment with such devilish names living in it? The flora has chain fruit and ironwood listed in its catalogue of heartless plants. The fauna has vultures circling over you by day and vampire bats dive-bombing you at night. There is no siren call of the sea here. There is just a vast, mournful pan of emptiness where anything sentient resents anything else that's alive. Satan's sauna is what I call it. Every sun-scoured scrap of fauna has barbs, hooks or thorns. They want to rip and rend you, snag and splinter you. Every sun-seared excuse for an animal has poison, paw or claw. They're not as discriminating. They just want to eat you. The prince of darkness himself could not conjure up such a malignant sorcery, a blasphemous buffet, of grotesque life.

SENSATIONS- It's the sensations that let you know you're dying. Your **skin feels like it's been stabbed** by a million sun-spears and **scraped by sandpaper**. Your **tongue is cloven to the roof of your mouth**. It's like there's a dry, leathery in-sole wagging away at the back of your throat. Your throat itself has **the sensation that a reticulated python is trying to squeeze** the life out of it. Even your **eyes feel like they've melted into the back of your mind**, making everything seem mirage-like. Sand is your enemy. It **burns your feet raw**, it **stings the eyes** and it acts as a surrogate for pain because nothing else fills up your daily thoughts like it. Every step feels like a marathon, every second a day. At any moment you expect Armageddon to descend and sweep you away. You stumble and totter, as shriveled and contorted as the plant life around you. A nebula of wavy radiation surrounds you until you start believing that its one big field of it you're going through. At night, the mercury screams in agony as it plummets to its nadir. It's as cold as a ghoul's soul. Your **body trembles** feverishly and your **teeth rattle** as numbness spreads. Eventually, an overwhelming desire to give up and go to sleep forever overtakes you. Your will to live is steadily sapped away. I'm not quite at that point yet.

SOUNDS- I've heard it said that the desert is crypt-quiet, motionless and soundless. It's true to a large degree but only because your mind feels like it's taken a fistful of tranquillizers, dumbing the brain. Like any madness, there are moments of clarity. You have to really concentrate to become aware of the desert noises. Listen carefully and it's a veritable monkey's cage of maddening sounds. Every animal here is **screeching** or **shambling**, **screaming** or **shuffling**. Those who fall victim to the deserts cruel ways get eviscerated by a fat fang or scavenging beak. Scorpions **scuttle** and snakes **hiss** and **slither** while they go about their grisly business of desert survival. When night descends, the sonar-**ping** of marauding vampire bats **lacerates** the air. Deadly eyes glitter and shut as the night mammals take over. Their eerie **howls** and **harrowing** grunts fill up the loneliness you feel in your soul. Then you sense they may be **stalking** you. Hatred of them and their ill-begotten ilk takes over. Any sound of **sniffing** nostril, any **shuddering** bush becomes a threat to your existence. You begin to **slink** and **skulk** just like those around you. The constant paranoia is enough to unhinge the most obdurate of minds.

SIGHTS- Natures laws have been overthrown in the desert. It's an orgy of wanton violence between its denizens, all of whom have been disfigured and crippled by their attempts to live there. The gene pool of life has been corrupted beyond repair. You will only ever get to see five colours in the desert. The dominant one is the sand which pollutes the earth with an unending plain of **wasteland-brown**. Occasionally, reluctantly, it offers up a contorted, **viper-green** cactus, spiny of skin and bitter to the eye. Look up and you will see a burning, **sulfur-yellow** sun, resentful of life and soaking the land with its spite. The night brings with it a cloak of **despair-black**. In your final indignity, the stars appear, beautiful and scattered. Their shining brilliance is **mockery-silver**. They are a condescending reminder that for you there is no hope, no succour to be found in this melting pot of insanity. You are alone, abandoned and doomed. You are battling against nature itself and you're aware that no one has ever won that particular bout. Tomorrow at dawn a colourless heat haze will blur out the background and your vision will become myopic again. Your mind will draw in on itself like bowstrings and if you had to describe the haze you would say that it's a wobbly, shimmering mirror of your own death.

SMELLS- There is one main smell in the desert. It is the smell of your own death and it follows you everywhere. It's **ungodly** and it's as **virulent** as the heat itself. **Cloying** and **sticky**, the multitudinous seas incarnadine could not wash it away. It wafts and wallows, billows and blows all around you, your only ever-present companion besides hopelessness. There are more smells to be detected in this a la carte menu of death. Fear pervades from every pore and its smell is nearly as **fetid** and **pungent**. Mingled in amongst them is the **noxious** swirl of body odour. It is **rancid** and **rank** and makes you want to vomit with disgust. Around you, the scanty scrub-bushes smell **flamed** and **fried**. An unhealthy fume of burning sand, as stuffy as old **car exhausts**, rises up like a fog and oscillates just below your nose. It never seems to go away, so much so that you think that the gaseous emanations are part of the landscape. The smells seem as if they are chained inside your nostrils. Every breath you take is a living agony. It's like drowning in a stew-pot of smoky **cordite** and melting **asphalt**. You feel like you can't go on and your brain swells up until it feels as **grilled** and **griddled** as the air around you.

TASTES- There is nothing **ambrosial** or **appetizing** about the tastes of the desert. Defeat is the last taste on your palate. The only thing **lavish** or **extravagant** is the manner of your death. There's nothing **mouth-watering** as there's no water to be drank. There's nothing **opulent** or **tantalizing** to be had. There's nothing at all for you to do except to bow down to the blasphemous desire of the desert to kill you. I'm tired now. I'm sick of the stumbling and the staggering, the tottering and the trembling. I'm sick of the cracked lips and the kidney-skewering pain of dehydration. Most of all, I'm sick of life. The sand is burning my head now for I have fallen for the last time. My large, Berber-brown eyes can feel the tears. I've had enough of survival in Satan's solarium. Seventeen years as a camel in this inferno of fire and fumes was just too much to ask of me.

ONOMATOPOEIA

Onomatopoeia is when the meaning of a word is obvious from its sound. Its main purpose is to recreate the sounds of the scene the writer conjures up. By using onomatopoeia, the reader is catapulted into this world without having a choice. Next to colour, it is the most important sensory weapon in the armoury of a descriptive writer. Murmurs of wind in the trees can become the howling tempests of winter with the flick of a pen. That is the beauty of using onomatopoeia; the writer can control the atmosphere and the mood of the passage through his/her choice of words. The grids underneath give some of the most effective sounds and formulas for evoking an atmosphere in a battle scene.

SOFT WINDS IN ESCALATING VOLUME	LOUD WINDS IN ESCALATING VOLUME	COLLISION WORDS WITH 3 SYLLABLES
breathing	mewling	battering
exhaling	shrieking	bludgeoning
sighing	screaming	bombarding
soughing	screeching	clobbering
whispering	wailing	fracturing
murmuring	snarling	pummelling
suspiring	howling	rupturing
whimpering	yowling	splintering
gasping	keening	sundering
puffing	caterwauling	walloping

A good technique is to start off a battle scene with a placid scene. It could be a cloudless day with a gentle breeze. Euphony can be used for the wind. It may be exhaling or whispering. Then as the scene unfolds, the clouds begin to boil and the sun is blotted out. The soldiers begin to get nervous as the enemy appears. This was alluded to in the pathetic fallacy section earlier. The words get steadily louder and harsher as the battle commences. This is called **cacophony**, also known as **dissonance**.

The key ingredient is to have a word bank planned beforehand. If the words are increasing in intensity, it will give a good climax to the story. I have seen articles and books where other writers have argued against this. They probably do not have to sit an important exam where they are judged on what they can write in a short space of time!

Cacophony is the use of loud, harsh or jarring sounds in a passage of writing. It is the opposite of euphony and it is particularly useful when describing battle scenes, storms or thunder and lightning. Its purpose is to recreate the mood and sounds of a tempestuous scene. The grid shows the difference between the dissonance (cacophony) of the top grid and the more mellow effect of the bottom grid. The phonics does not change in the 'ng' column, but there is a huge difference between the harsh and the soft sounds. By putting them all in a sentence, one can see the difference in impact and noise they create.

SENTENCE 1: "The armour was **clanging** as the steel tips of the **fizzing** arrows were **clanking** into them".

SENTENCE 2: "The armour was **dinging** as the wooden tips of the **strumming** arrows were **chinking** into them".

The first sentence is strident and resonant. The second one has a musical lilt, a tinny ping if you like. By deconstructing different sounds and phonics, a teacher or educator can demonstrate clearly the link between sound and mood in an essay.

HARSH 'ng' SOUNDS	FAST 'zz' SOUNDS	DEEP 'nk' SOUNDS
clanging	buzzing	clanking
clangourous	fizzing	clonking
gong	fizzling	clunking
jangling	sizzling	plunking
twanging	whizzing	thunking
SOFT 'ng' SOUNDS	**FAST DOUBLE LETTERS**	**MUSICAL 'nk' SOUNDS**
dinging	stru**mm**ing arrows	chinking
jingling	thru**mm**ing arrows	clinking
pinging	whi**rr**ing arrows	plinking
ringing	z**oo**ming arrows	tinkling

Consonance is the repetition of final consonant sounds in a sentence or passage of writing. Using words ending in 'ng', for example', would lend a metallic quality to the sentence. Most typically, words ending with a 's' are used to lend a sinister or fearful mood to the passage. **"The insidious mist creeps towards the nervous hills"**. The use of five words ending with a 's' make it a clear example.

Because there's a hissing quality throughout the sentence, it is also an example of **sibilance.**

DESCRIBING BATTLE SCENES

SKY COLOUR

LEVEL 1	LEVEL 2	LEVEL 3	LEVEL 4	LEVEL 5	OTHERS
bat-black	cauldron-black	pagan-black	corbie-black	Barabbas-black	
cobra-black	carrion-black	profane-black	carnal-black	Beelzebub-black	

1. A *scar* of bright light hung in the bat-black sky.
2. A *gash* of radiant light broke through the cauldron-black sky.
3. A *fracture* of birthstone-bright light peeped through the pagan-black sky.
4. A *rupture* of moonstone-yellow light appeared in the carnal-black sky.
5. A *lesion* of lodestar-bright light illuminated the benighted sky.

BLOOD COLOUR

berry-red	poppy-red	magma-red	balefire-red	hellacious-red	
mercury-red	brazier-red	molten-red	brimstone-red	Titian-red	

1. Berry-red blood *squirted* from our wounds.
2. Brazier-red blood *sprayed* from our wounds.
3. Molten-red blood *splashed* from our open wounds.
4. Balefire-red blood *splattered* from our gaping wounds.
5. Titian-red blood *spurted* from our wounds as men wailed and screamed.

BATTLE SOUNDS

banging	clobbering	smashing	carving	hacking	
bashing	clubbing	smiting	cleaving	hewing	
battering	clunking	pounding	blasting	lashing/gashing	

Writing with Stardust

| beating | crashing | pummelling | bludgeoning | mangling/gouging | |

1. We were battering and beating against our enemy under a **sunless** sky.
2. We were clobbering and clubbing against their shield wall under a **moonless** sky.
3. We were pounding and pummelling their defences under a **beamless** sky.
4. We were carving and cleaving towards the centre of their army under a **rayless** sky.
5. We were mangling and gashing their serried ranks under a **starless** sky.

MISSILE SOUNDS

buzzing and fizzing	shrilling and sissing	puling and purling	trembling and thrumming	skirling and sizzling	
fizzling and frizzling	zipping and hissing	rasping and keening	whizzing and whistling	whining and wailing	

1. A **storm** of arrows was buzzing and fizzing through the sky.
2. A **blizzard** of spears was shrilling and sissing through the sky.
3. A **tempest** of lances was rasping and keening through the basalt-black sky.
4. A **maelstrom** of pig stickers was whizzing and whistling through the benzene-black sky.
5. A **windstorm** of fire arrows was skirling and sizzling through the bitumen-black sky.

CRIES OF PAIN

screaming screeching	snarling squealing	roaring mewling	groaning yowling	bawling bellowing	
wailing whimpering	sobbing snivelling	blubbering choking	yelping yammering	keening caterwauling	

1. Men were screaming and screeching as the ground became **slippery with sludge**.
2. Men were snarling and squealing as the ground became **greasy with gore**.
3. Men were blubbering and choking as the battleground became **slimy with intestines**.
4. Men were groaning and yowling as the battlefield became **slick with innards**.
5. The theatre of death filled up with keening and caterwauling sounds as the sodden earth became **oily with ichor**.

SOUNDS OF METAL

chiming	clinking	jingling	clattering	clanging	
chinking	ringing	jangling	clanking	clangourous	

1. Our harnesses were chinking and dinging under the **boiling** sky.

2. Our swords were clinking and clashing under the **churning** sky.

3. Our chain armour was jingling and tinkling under the **turbulent,** cellar-black sky.

4. Our axes were clattering and clanking into their wooden shields under the **roiling**, doom-laden sky.

5. Our weapons were clanging and clangourous under the **seething**, spite-filled sky.

PLURAL NOUNS FOR MONSTERS

a sea of enemies	a flood of monsters	a host of ogres	a hive of cannibals	a plague of hellhounds	
a swarm of opponents	a legion of trolls	a horde of beasts	a throng of goblins	an infestation of orcs	

1. Our bones were **breaking and popping** as a sea of enemies crashed into us.

2. Our bones were **snapping and shattering** as a flood of monsters broke our lines.

3. Our bones were **cracking and crunching** as a horde of beasts smashed into us.

4. Our bones were **fracturing and rupturing** as a throng of goblins hurtled into us.

5. Our bones were **splitting and splintering** as a plague of hellhounds careered into us.

SMELL

vile	sickly	noxious	pungent	mildew	
ungodly	septic	nauseating	putrefying	mordant	

1. The ground was **glazed with gizzards** and a vile smell rose up from it.

2. The ground was **burnished with entrails** and a sickly odour rose up from it.

3. The ground was **lubricated with guts** and a nauseating waft arose from it.

4. The battleground was **anointed with bowels**. The putrefying stench of a thousand battles seemed to come from it.

5. The effluvium of death was all around us. The battlefield had been *baptised in blood* and the bitter, mordant perfume of corpses emanated from it.

SENSATION

eye-popping	head-clasping	skin-crawling	bone-rattling	bladder-emptying	
heart-thumping	marrow-freezing	spine-chilling	blood-curdling	bowel-loosening	

1. Our new armour was *flashing like moon fire*, but it was an eye-popping moment,
2. Our lances *sparkled like dew gleam*, but it was a marrow-freezing moment.
3. Our new shields were *gleaming like star flame*, but it was a spine-chilling moment.
4. The dewy grass *flickered like diamond flame* as a blood-curdling howl rent the air.
5. Our spear tips *glinted like wicked hoar frost*, but the screams of the enemy were bowel-loosening.

TASTE

salty	acrid	tangy	brackish	cerulean	
saline	vinegary	tart	briny	coppery	

1. A *jet* of blood surged into the air. It tasted salty.
2. A *fountain* of blood soaked my face. It tasted vinegary.
3. A *geyser* of blood showered into the air. It tasted tangy.
4. A *spritz* of blood spouted into the air. It tasted brackish.
5. A *wellspring* of blood sluiced into the air. It tasted coppery.

LEVEL 1: BASIC SENTENCES

1. The sky was **cobra-black**. **SKY COLOUR**
2. **Mercury-red** blood drizzled to the ground. **BLOOD COLOUR**
3. Our enemies were **banging and bashing** at our lines. **BATTLE SOUNDS**
4. Our fire arrows were **fizzing and fizzling** through the air. **MISSILE SOUNDS**
5. Their men were **wailing and whimpering** in pain. **CRIES OF PAIN**
6. Our armour was **chiming** as the horses galloped. **SOUND OF METAL**

7. **A swarm** of opponents attacked us. **PLURAL NOUNS**

8. The smell of battle was **ungodly**. **SMELL**

9. The battle was **heart-thumping**. **SENSATION**

10. The **saline** taste of blood was in my mouth. **TASTE**

LEVEL 2: A BASIC PARAGRAPH

The sky was **carrion-black**. **Poppy-red** blood drizzled from our wounds. The trolls were **clunking** axes and **crashing** war hammers against our shields. Arrows were **zipping and hissing** through the air. Some of our men were **sobbing and snivelling** with fear. Swords were **ringing** against each other. **A legion of trolls** attacked the centre of our lines. The **septic** smell of death hung over the battlefield. It was a battle of **head-clasping** horror. The **acrid** taste of blood rose up in our mouths.

LEVEL 3: MIRROR SENTENCES

1 The sky was **profane-black**. **(Creating atmosphere)**

2 Our **cold** hands gripped our **cold**, steel swords. **(Repetition)**

3 The **w**ind **w**hipped at our faces. **(Alliteration)**

4 We looked at the **sea of monsters** that surrounded us. **(Metaphor)**

5 Their spears glinted wickedly. **We were afraid. (Using a personal response)**

6 Their feet **stamped** as they **roared** up at us. **(Onomatopoeia)**

7 **"Fire!"** our commander screamed. **(Using direct speech)**

8 A **storm of arrows (Metaphor) whizzed** and **fizzed** into the night. **(Onomatopoeia)**

9 **Ember-red** blood **(Using colour) gushed (Onomatopoeia)** from the monsters.

10 They surged forward. It was **like being attacked by a swarm of insects. (Simile)**

11 Their iron ladders **clanked** off the castle walls. **(Onomatopoeia)**

12 They all had **bulbous eyes (Character description)** and they blazed **magma-red** with hatred. **(Using colour)**

13 Our **teeth chattered (Sense of sensation)** and our **spines tingled** with fear. **(Sense of sensation)**

14 The swishe**s** and hisse**s** of sword**s** slashing through the air made the battle seem more perilou**s**. **(Consonance)**

15 His sword rose. I fell. **(Short syntax for dramatic effect)**

LEVEL 4: MIRROR SENTENCES

1 The sky was **damnation-black**. **(Better diction)**

2 Our **cold** hands gripped our **gelid** swords. **(Better diction)**

3 The wind **screamed** and **slashed** at our faces. **(Alliteration and pathetic fallacy)**

4 A **plague of monsters (Better metaphor)** teemed beneath our feet at **the castle walls**. **(Establishing location quicker than before)**

5 Their spears glittered and glowed under the ghostly moonlight. **(Assonance)**

6 Their feet **thundered** on the valley's cold floor as they **bellowed** up at us. **(Onomatopoeia)**

7 Our commander screamed: "**Fire!**" and we loosed our arrows. **(Better command of syntax)**

8 A **blizzard of arrows (Metaphor) buzzed** and **hummed** into the shroud of black sky. **(Onomatopoeia)**

9 **Molten-red** blood **(Better colour) sluiced (Onomatopoeia)** from the deadly wounds the arrows caused.

10 The monsters swarmed forward **like a plague of ravenous locusts. (Better simile)**

11 Their iron ladders were **thunking** and **clanging** off the castle walls. **(Better onomatopoeia)**

12 They all had **saurian eyes** and they were **festering with hatred** for us. **(More creative description)**

13 Our **hearts pounded** against our rib cages and our **neck hairs felt like pins** with the terror of it all. **(Better expression of sensation)**

14 The slithering sounds of thousands of swords being unsheathed were frightening. **(Consonance)**

15 It was carnage. **(Short syntax for dramatic effect)**

LEVEL 5: MIRROR SENTENCES

The starless sky was casket-black and **brooding**. **(Using pathetic fallacy)** Even the clouds seemed morose. Gelid hands **clasped** algid steel as we gazed **upon** our foe. The cold, north wind **keened** and **mewled** through both the valley and the souls of our men. **(Four archaic words)**

The clouds cleared. Their spears glimmered cruelly under the eerie moon. Its phantom flame sent ribbons of chrysalis-silver light spilling onto the upraised shields of our men. **(Assonance)** The monsters swarmed and swayed below us like corn in a field, yet it seemed there were **more of them than a thousand bushels could hold. (Hyperbole)** Our commander raised our **p**roud **p**ennant aloft in defiance. **(Alliteration)** It represented **our** dreams, **our** lives and **our** salvation. **(Triplication and symbolism)** If it was taken, it would mean we were dead.

They crashed upon the castle walls as our commander screamed: "Fire!" in desperation**. (Better syntax)** Their iron-shod feet clapped off the frozen ground **like the rumbling of thunder. (Simile)** A **tempest of** wicked, barbed fire arrows **(Metaphor) s**oared into the **s**ombre **s**ky. **(Alliteration)** They **sizzed** and **sizzled (Onomatopoeia)** before hitting their targets. **Fountains of magma-red blood (Metaphor using hyperbole)** sprayed into the air. It was butchery. **(Short syntax for dramatic effect)** We hoped that we would survive the day. **(Finish with hope or despair)**

PLANNING WITH THE GRIDS: LEVEL 1

I am asked regularly by my students **how** to plan an essay. The answer to that is that it takes time and practise. Da Vinci, for example, didn't start his career by painting the roofs of chapels and masterpieces. He had to serve his apprenticeship and perfect his craft. The real question is how do you **start** to plan an essay? This book attempts to provide an answer. Planning any level of an English assignment should involve some thought. That is why some writers like to be labelled as 'wordsmiths'. It infers that the thought processes are a metaphorical lump of metal. How does that lump of metal become a silver pen? It needs to be heated (collecting images), smelted (forming sentences), cooled down (sequencing ideas) and forged into the shape of a pen (paragraph structure). That doesn't mean the process is finished. The pen may not work, even though it looks like the finished product. It may need to be re-heated and re-forged (a redraft). Finally, both the pen and the essay are ready. 'Writing with Stardust' provides a unique way to get the process started, to fire up the forge, so to speak. The best approach is to pick a chapter and take one word from each of the ten Level 1 grids. Then get the student to rearrange them in sequence. Once this is done, they may then put them into sentences. This is what it would look like for the **MIST** chapter.

MIST			**RAIN**	**FLOODS**
ghost-grey mist	shreds of mist	encircled	spraying rain	plump drops
voiceless and heartless	crept over the ground	smoky and steamy mist	airy rain	tea-brown, boiling river

They should then form **five sentences** using these words.

1. The ghost-grey mist was voiceless and heartless.
2. Shreds of mist crept over the ground.
3. The smoky and steamy mist encircled the mountain.
4. The airy, spraying rain banished the mist.
5. Plump drops of rain fell then and the river became tea-brown and boiling.

This is the start of the process. If they are not capable of this, they should be encouraged to practise it until it becomes second nature to them. They will not be able to sequence paragraphs if they cannot sequence sentences so there is little point in moving ahead.

If they are capable of sequencing sentences, they are ready to move on to the next stage. You could then ask them to introduce a character from the **FEMALES** chapter. They should only use Level 1 again until they are comfortable with this process. The grid should look something like this;

FEMALES

an hour glass figure	a bumblebee waist	silky eyelashes	shining, halo-white teeth	dreamy, bliss-blue eyes
elf thin	glowing skin	a pointy nose	sunrise-gold hair	puffy lips

They can then repeat the process by putting the words into five sentences.
1. She was elf thin with an hour glass figure.
2. She had a bumblebee waist with glowing skin.
3. Her silky eyelashes fluttered above a pointy nose.
4. Her shining, halo-white teeth gleamed as much as her sunrise-gold hair.
5. Her dreamy, bliss-blue eyes were as attractive as her puffy lips.

The materials are now there for the introduction to an essay. In this case, it may be the day the narrator fell in love with someone for the first time. By fusing both character description and the natural surroundings, it should provide a narrative that entertains the reader and keeps the plot flowing.

SAMPLE INTRODUCTION TO AN ESSAY

The day I fell in love was also the day I died. The weather forecast was for a bright day with mild weather. The girl's name was Rebecca and I had arranged to meet her by a bench near the riverbank. She was elf thin with an hour glass figure and I was attracted to her. Her bumblebee waist and glowing skin appealed to me also. I had never even talked to her and it was her friends who had set up the blind date. Although I thought that it might be a practical joke, I decided to meet her anyway.

As always, the forecasters were wrong. The sky was clay-grey and I could see mist in the distance. It was voiceless and heartless as shreds of it moved over the ground. Rising up, the smoky and steamy mist encircled the mountains. Just then I heard a shout. It was Rebecca. My heart leaped as I saw her sunrise-gold hair flash in the pale light. Her shining, halo-white teeth gleamed as she broke into a smile. She was walking towards me along the slippery river bank. An airy, spraying rain started to fall, but I barely noticed. As she came closer, I nearly melted into her dreamy, bliss-blue eyes. The sight of her puffy lips parting into a bigger smile felt like an electric current was running through my heart. Then disaster struck.

With a cry of surprise, she suddenly disappeared from my view! She shouted again but this time it was one of distress. Running towards her, I could see her head bobbing up and down as the fast current swept her away. The river was tea-brown and boiling with anger. Plump drops of rain started to fall as if to add to its rage. I didn't even think of the danger. I plunged into the foaming river. It was icy, dark and tasted like mud when I hit the bottom and took in a mouthful of water. Gasping and choking, I rose to the surface and swung my arms as much as I could. In between waves of water blocking my view, I could see Rebecca just in front of me. I thrashed my arms even harder.

Just as I was about to reach her, she hit a tree branch that was sticking out from the bank. I swept past her with a howl of shock. The river became wider, faster and deeper as I rounded a bend. I felt like a skittle as I was tossed up and down. At one point, my feet were facing up to the sky. I died inside then. I knew my time was up. I saw a bright light and faded away when my head hit a branch under the water. The doctors told me later that if Rebecca hadn't let go of the tree to save me, I would have died. They said she was very brave. They never said that about me but they gave me many strange looks. When it got around the school that I had been saved by a girl I had jumped in to rescue, I had to put up with years of bad jokes.

I never talked to Rebecca after that day. She was removed from the school by her parents. I have never had a nightmare about my experience, but I dream every night of once more meeting the girl with the sunrise-gold hair.

The story above had some very clear objectives from the start. The objectives were that:

1. It had a dramatic hook sentence.

2. It had a clear paragraph structure.

3. It used a character description with a theme of love.

4. It had pathetic fallacy by using nature to reflect a characters mood.

5. It gave the tastes and sensations of the cold river.

6. It used human emotions of fear and stress.

7. It had a plot with a twist.

8. The diction would be easy to use and make the story flow.

By keeping the objectives simple, a student is ready to plan a full essay using paragraphs.

THE MIST: THE RAIN: A FLOOD RIVER

COLOUR

LEVEL 1	LEVEL 2	LEVEL 3	LEVEL 4	LEVEL 5	OTHERS
ghost-grey	spook-grey	phantom-grey	phantasm-grey	wraith-grey	
ghoul-grey	spectre-grey	poltergeist-grey	fantasm-grey	apparition-grey	

1. The ghoul-grey mist was *as thick as pea soup*.
2. The spectre-grey mist was *as foul as a witch's broth*.
3. The phantom-grey mist was *as vile as the devil's brew*.
4. Fetlocks of phantasm-grey mist hovered *like a sorcerer's smoke*.
5. Waves of wraith-grey mist coiled and writhed *like a conjuror's smoke*.

LACK OF SOUND

voiceless and heartless	wordless and passionless	tongue less and spineless	soundless and soulless	fathomless and friendless	
noiseless and bloodless	lifeless and motherless	rootless and breathless	echoless and emotionless	kinless and kith less	

1. The mist was voiceless and heartless as it *draped* the mountain.
2. The mist was wordless and passionless as it *sheathed* the mountain.
3. The mist was rootless and breathless as it *mantled* the forest.
4. The mist was soundless and soulless as it slyly *festooned* the wood.
5. The Undead-grey mist was fathomless and friendless as it *garlanded* the cliffs.

SHAPE

shreds	rags	tentacles	fingers	membranes	

Writing with Stardust

| shavings | ribbons | tassels | fetters | miasmas | |

1. Shreds of mist *passed* through the fields.
2. Ribbons of wavy mist *puffed* through the meadow.
3. Tassels of cunning mist *pilfered* through the dale.
4. Fingers of wriggling mist *phantomed* through the forest.
5. Miasmas of mist seemed to *percolate* up from the steaming earth.

.

ACTION

| crept over | grabbed at | clung to | clutched at | fastened itself | |
| crawled over | grasped at | clenched the | clasped itself | fettered itself | |

1. **Threads** of wavy mist crept over the ground.
2. **Splinters** of sly mist grabbed at the trees.
3. **Tatters** of sneaky mist clenched the ship's mast.
4. **Wisps** of wily mist clutched at the grass as they passed over.
5. **Sheets** of insidious mist fettered themselves to the mountain and strangled it in silence.

ARCHAIC WORDS

| encircled | enfolded | enrobed | entwined | enwreathed | |
| enwrapped | enclasped | enlaced | ensnared | enwrought | |

1. **Loops** of mist encircled the mountain.
2. **Coils** of mist enfolded the mountain.
3. **Nooses** of mist enlaced the haughty mountain.
4. The glowering mountain was *corralled* and ensnared by the crafty mist.
5. The stately mountain was *lassoed* and enwreathed by hanks of mist.

ADJECTIVES FOR MIST

| smoky and steaming | fumy and filmy | sorcerous illusory | evanescent ephemeral | brumous and nebulous | |
| trance-like | hazy and | ethereal and | vaporous and | unearthly and | |

| mirage-like | gauzy | gossamer-fragile | diaphanous | otherworldly | |

1. The steaming mist **lingered** in the air.
2. The hazy, gauzy mist **lounged** in the air.
3. The sorcerous and illusory mist **leisured** in the air.
4. The evanescent and ephemeral mist **loitered** in the dead air.
5. Furrows of brumous and nebulous mist **languished** in the deathlike air.

RAIN SOUNDS

| spraying | susurrating | spitting | shredding | sizzling | |
| showering | sissing | sibilant | seething | sluicing | |

1. The rain was spraying through the **screen** of mist.
2. The rain was susurrating through the **shroud** of mist.
3. The rain was sibilant and ripped through the **plume** of mist.
4. The rain was seething and shredded through the **pall** of milk-white mist.
5. The rain was sizzling and sluiced through the **spume** of spirit-grey mist.

LIGHT RAIN

| airy rain | mist-like | droplets of | dewdrops of | drizzling rain | |
| aeriform | sprinkling | pearls of | teardrops of | mizzling rain | |

1. The airy rain came from the *filmy* clouds above me.
2. The sprinkling rain came from the *fibrous* clouds above me.
3. Pearls of light rain came from the *furrow* of cloud above my head.
4. Teardrops of tepid rain drifted down from the *veil* of clouds above me.
5. The mizzling rain was warm and tinkled down from the *vellum* of cloud above.

HEAVY RAIN

| plump drops of | swollen drops of | soaking rain | icy rain | silver nails of | |
| ploppy drops | pregnant | saturating | stinging rain | silver bullets | |

	drops of	rain		of	

1. The plump raindrops were *as hot and hissing as the devil's spit*.
2. The swollen raindrops were *as thick and stinging as a troll's spittle*.
3. The saturating rain was *as fiery and splattering as witch-spit*.
4. The stinging rain was *as sibilant and sinister as a warlock's hiss*.
5. Silver nails of rain pinged and sissed off the corrugated roof *like a dragon's, dripping spit*.

FLOODED RIVER COLOURS

tea-brown and boiling	whiskey-brown and sloshing	brandy-brown and roiling	cognac-brown and foaming	mocha-brown and lathering	
bog-brown and broiling	turf-brown and slushing	peat-brown and rumbling	estuary-brown and frothy	molasses-brown and threshing	

1. The tea-brown river was boiling as it **carved** through the ravine.
2. The whiskey-brown river was sloshing as it **gashed** the river's banks.
3. The brandy-brown flood was rumbling as it **gouged** out chunks of the bank.
4. The cognac-brown floodwater was foaming as it **hacked** through the meadow.
5. The mocha-brown torrent was lathering itself into a rage. It made a sound like bottled thunder as it trundled and **slashed** through the valley.

LEVEL 1: BASIC SENTENCES

1. The mist was **ghost-grey. COLOUR**
2. It was **noiseless and bloodless. LACK OF SOUND**
3. **Shavings** of mist passed over the field. **SHAPE**
4. It **crawled** over the still wheat. **ACTION**
5. It **enwrapped** the scarecrow. **ARCHAIC WORDS**
6. It was **mirage-like** as it moved. **ADJECTIVES**
7. The rain was **showering** the field. **RAIN SOUNDS**
8. It was thin and **aeriform** rain. **LIGHT RAIN**

9. The **ploppy** drops came later. **HEAVY RAIN**
10. The river was **broiling and bog-brown. FLOOD RIVERS**

LEVEL 2: A BASIC PARAGRAPH

The mist was **spook-grey**. It was **lifeless and motherless**. **Rags** of the mist tickled the lake as it passed. It **grasped at** the calm water. It moved on and **enclasped** the shrubs. It looked **fumy and filmy** in the weak light of the morning. The rain began **sissing** off the pond. The rain seemed **mist-like** also as it came down in thin sheets. It became heavier and **pregnant drops** of the rain arrived. After hours of this, the river was **turf-brown and slushing**.

LEVEL 3: CREATIVE PARAGRAPHS

The tranquil valley was swaddled in a veil of **poltergeist-white** mist. It was eerily silent in the valley and the reason was obvious. The deathly vapour didn't lick the valley's cold floor as the wind was known to do. Its **tongue less** form wouldn't allow it to. Instead, it warped nature by using its **spineless tentacles** to trail around everything. It drifted and ghosted, glided and dangled. Then it pounced. Once it was sure it had conjured up enough of its milky white substance, it **clung to** and **enrobed** everything it could. Nothing was spared. It snagged and snared every crag and tree without mercy.

Although it looked **ethereal and gossamer-fragile**, it packed a punch far above its weightlessness. It writhed and coiled with delight, its ghostly scarves wrapping the valley in a maze of mist. Then its age-old enemy arrived to banish it into nothingness. Darts of icy rain came **spitting** from the sky. They hissed and swished, shredding the veil into collars of isolated steam. Increasing in intensity, fat **droplets** of soaking rain purged the valley of any remaining mist. The incessant rain swelled the river, bursting its banks. It turned **peat-brown** immediately, **rumbling** through the valley's rocky caverns. This time, the rain had won.

LEVELS 4 AND 5: COMPLEX WRITING

A labyrinth of **fantasm-grey** mist hung over the forest. It seemed as if it had arisen as part of the forest's wet breath. Hovering like voodoo vapour in the arcane light of the morning, it was motionless as it surveyed the trees beneath. Like an apparition one might see over an ancient barrow, it was more than air and less than flesh and blood. **Kinless and kith less**, it wove itself together, increasing in density. When it was satisfied its form could **entwine** the trees, it began to descend, **clasping itself** onto their leafy heads. **Fetters** of the **diaphanous** mist fastened themselves around the wood, leaving no tree unharmed. Although it was incorporeal, it managed to fade the mossy trees into a grim-grey reflection of itself. Like unholy incense, it wafted and spirited through the forest, swathing everything in its vaporous patina.

As wild and fantastic as a chimera, it grew in substance and intensity, steaming with its own spite. The forest took on an unearthly aspect. It was as if this devil's tattoo had been designed to hide its beauty. Nature doesn't allow anything to be immutable, however. A heavy **dewdrop** of rain was the first sign that the mist had gone too far. Then a drizzle came, followed by a deluge. The rain increased until it was **seething and sizzling**. Raindrops seared the mist, ripping it apart with its **stinging, silver bullets**. The forest was hissing like the dripping saliva of a demon. It lost its otherworldly aspect, gradually taking form again. When the last shred of mist had disappeared, a flood river raced through the forest, as if to celebrate nature's verve and vigour. **Threshing** and echoing into the distance, its sound was the final death knell for the silent mist.

PLANNING A LEVEL 5

Planning a Level 5 essay may take a different type of approach. In the 'Waterfall' chapter, for example, I wanted to use the zoom narration technique that I talked about on page 4. To do this, a waterfall has to be broken down into its three main features: sound, motion and appearance.

SOUND: The aim was to recapture both the loud, stentorian sounds and soft, musical effect of a waterfall. To do this I would need a mixture of **cacophony** and **euphony**.

MOTION: The objective was to recreate the smooth, eel-like quality of a waterfall as it slid over the rock. A mixture of euphonious **similes** and **metaphors** were required for that.

APPEARANCE: If possible, I also wanted to capture the mirage-like and hallucinatory effect of the spray as it glimmered in the light. The use of selective **diction** and lucid **imagery** were the main focus here.

Then it was just a case of deconstructing the passage down to its most basic component-words.

Introduction- The distance of sound: humming, buzzing, tingle.

Paragraph 1- Sounds increasing in volume: growling, rumbling, foamed, cacophonous, thunderclap.

Paragraph 1- Sounds of the infinity pool: rushed, roiling, bubbling, boiling, churning.

Paragraph 2- Creative sounds for water: swoosh-plunk, hiss-plop, salvo, slushiness, slobbering.

Paragraph 2- 'S' verbs to recreate the flow: streamed, smooth, spilled, slid.

Paragraph 2- The sound of bells: chiming, chinking, tinkling, pinged, plinked.

Paragraph 3- The sunlight on the spray: a-glitter, sparkling, flickering, shimmering, dazzling.

Paragraph 3- Five words for surreal: trance-like, dreamy, illusory, mirage, mystique.

Conclusion- humming repeated.

Negative words not included: slithered, serpentine, snaked, salacious, sneaky.

Whether a student tries to use the grids or word clusters like this, both methods are highly successful in imparting a love of English. He or she will also get to love the texture of the language as they are working from a pattern that they can relate to. It is always better for an educator to show **how to do it** rather than tell a student what to do. By working from the basics upwards, a student can empower himself/herself to enjoy English and to thrive at it.

THUNDER AND LIGHTNING

COLOUR

LEVEL 1	LEVEL 2	LEVEL 3	LEVEL 4	LEVEL 5	OTHERS
raven-black	cowl-black	witch soul-black	abyss-black	heathen-black	
mamba-black	coven-black	devil heart black	succubus-black	blasphemous-black	

1. Lightning *flashed* and slashed through the mamba-black sky.
2. Lightning *flickered* and cackled in the coven-black sky.
3. Lightning *flared*. It seethed and streaked across the witch soul-black sky.
4. Lightning *flamed* in the sky. It whirred and whipped across the abyss-black clouds.
5. Lightning *enflamed* the heathen-black sky. It whimpered and wriggled like a wizard's whip before dying into nothingness.

SOUND

booming and blasting	clapping and bellowing	groaning and growling	roaring and rolling	sonorous and stentorian	
clanging and clanking	cracking and crashing	grumbling and rumbling	pealing and yowling	cacophonous clangorous	

1. The booming and blasting thunder burst **the cocoon of silence**.
2. The clapping and bellowing thunder ripped **the fragile veil of silence**.
3. The groaning and growling thunder fractured **the sacristy-still peace**.
4. **The mausoleum-quiet silence** was rent by the pealing and yowling thunder.
5. **The ecclesiastical silence** was blasted apart by the sonorous and stentorian thunder.

SHAPE

boiling skies	riotous skies	crumpling skies	moiling skies	turbulent skies	

| churning skies | rumpled skies | buckling skies | roiling skies | tumultuous skies | |

1. The boiling sky was **gun barrel-black**.

2. The riotous sky was **gunpowder-black**.

3. The crumpling, buckling sky was **thundercloud-black**.

4. The moiling and roiling skies were **midnight-black** and looming over us.

5. The turbulent skies were a ruinous, **vulcanite-black** and spoke of impending doom.

ACTION

explosion	rang	mournful	resonated	sombre
detonation	echoed	discordant	reverberated	sonic boom

1. An explosion of thunder tore split *the vault-like silence*.

2. Thunder echoed in the sky and shattered *the shrine-still silence*.

3. The mournful thunder tore *the womb-like silence* apart.

4. Thunder resonated in the sky and splintered *the tomb-like silence*. Then it faded into tintinnabulation.

5. *The cenotaph-still silence* was ruptured by the sonic boom of thunder. The aftershock hummed in the air long after it had died.

LIGHTNING COLOUR

star flame-gold	lustrous-gold	glitter-gold	foil-gold	gaslight-gold	
star blaze-gold	luminous-gold	gamboge-gold	fulvous-gold	God-goldened	

1. The *brilliant* lightning was star flame-gold.

2. The *radiant* lightning was lustrous-gold.

3. The *resplendent* lightning was glitter-gold.

4. The *scintillating* lightning flashed like foil-gold.

5. The *incandescent* lightning was a-blaze in its God-goldened glory.

SOUND

buzzed	hissed	fizzed	scorched	whizzed	
crackled	sissed	fizzled	seared	sizzled	

1. The **alien** lightning buzzed and crackled.
2. The **unearthly** lightning hissed and sissed.
3. The **otherworldly** lightning fizzed and fizzled across the sky.
4. The **arcane** lightning seared itself into flame and scorched across the sky.
5. The **eldritch** lightning sizzled itself into fire and whizzed across the sky.

SHAPE

branched	pronged	crooked	antlered	dendriform	
forked	veined	contorted	splayed	bifurcated	

1. The branched lightning was *shaped like twisted veins*.
2. The pronged lightning was *shaped like creeping capillaries*.
3. The crooked lightning was *shaped like misshapen plasma streams*.
3. The antlered lightning was *shaped like spread-eagled rivers of solar flame*.
5. The bifurcated lightning was *shaped like a witch's, warped whip*.

ACTION

blazing	humming	whining	slashing	razing	
purring	quivering	writhing	squealing	zigzagging	

1. The blazing lightning was *as crackly as frizzy, electrified hair*.
2. The quivering lightning was shaped *like a cat-o'-nine tails*.
3. The whining lightning was *as bright as the crawling cracks on stained glass*.
4. The squealing lightning was *as vitrified as the creeping cracks on a frozen pond*.
5. The zigzagging lightning was *like the ruinous cracks on crumbling mortar*.

COLD SEAS

a cold, steel-blue	an icy, polar-blue	a chilling, Siberian-blue	alpine-blue and algid	Antarctic-blue and frigid	
a cold, wintry-blue	an icy, Prussian-blue	arctic-blue and corpse-cold	iceberg-blue and Cossack-cold	glacier-blue and gelid	

1. The cold, steel-blue waves created a gentle *sea-song*.
2. The *soft symphony* of the sea was caused by the icy, Prussian-blue waves.
3. The slobbering waves were a chilling, Siberian-blue and created the *sand-song*.
4. The *wave-hum* was caused by the gentle roll of the alpine-blue sea.
5. The *wave-music* was caused by the salty tongue of the glacier-blue sea.

ANGRY SEAS

bashing the rocks	smacking the cliffs	buffeting the coast	spewing spite	whooshing waves	
battering the rocks	smashing the cliffs	bludgeoning the coast	suppurating hatred	walloping waves	

1. The *wild* sea was bashing the rocks.
2. The *savage* sea was smashing the cliffs.
3. The *barbarous* sea was buffeting the stoic coast.
4. The *feral* sea was spewing its bruised-blue spite against the adamant rock.
5. The *feckless* sea was walloping its brutal waves against the obdurate cliffs.

LEVEL 1: ADVANCED PARAGRAPHS

1. The sky was **raven-black**. **COLOUR**
2. It made a **clanging and clanking** noise. **SOUND**
3. It was **churning** with anger. **SHAPE**
4. The thunder **detonated** in the sky. **ACTION**
5. **Star blaze-gold lightning** flashed briefly. **COLOUR**

6. It was **whipping** with violence. **SOUND**

7. Its shape was **forked**. **SHAPE**

8. It was **purring** with energy. **ACTION**

9. It hit the **cold, wintry-blue sea**. **COLD SEAS**

10. The sea began **battering** the rocks. **ANGRY SEAS**

LEVEL 2: A BASIC PARAGRAPH

The sky was **cowl-black**. Thunder was **cracking and crashing** above our heads. The sky seemed **rumpled** as the clouds were deep and in different shades. Thunder **rang** out across the sky. **Luminous-gold** lightning flared once. It was **wriggling** towards the earth. It was **veined** and branched out. It began **humming** in a terrifying way. It blazed onto the **icy, polar-blue** sea. The angry sea began **smacking** the cliffs.

LEVEL 3: ADVANCED PARAGRAPHS

The gloomy sky was **as black as the devil's heart**. It was **grumbling and rumbling** with thunder like the stomachs of the Gods. The sky was **stirring** itself into frenzy, with pockets of grey and black clouds colliding. It pealed and yowled with bursts of brute force, making **discordant** noises all the while. The riotous sky was suddenly illuminated with **gamboge-gold** streaks. Lightning flared and **contorted** in forks of gold. It **screeched** and scorched towards the sea, **writhing** with pain.

The sea had been placid until then. It was **arctic-blue and corpse-cold**. Then the lightning slashed down and the sea began to boil. Its underbelly heaved up, causing huge waves to rise and crash down upon each other. They lurched across the sea in a mighty heap, dragging their foamy swells with them. Billowing and surging, the breakers cascaded towards the land. Enraged, they **bludgeoned** the cliffs with all their might, crashing into the stony walls. Unmoved, the cliffs stared back contemptuously. Then, when the sea had spent itself, they returned to their age-old dignity.

LEVEL 4: USING THE FORMULA

Each sentence contains the **shape,** the **sky,** the **sound,** the **colour,** the **brightness** and a **simile.**

1 **Antlered lightning** blazed in the **boiling,** autumn sky. It **buzzed** in its **beeswax-gold** splendour. The **brilliant lightning** was like a **cat-o'-nine tails.**

2 **Bifurcated lightning** electrified the **buckling,** autumn sky. It **crackled** in its **foil-gold** intensity. The **lambent lightning** was **as bright as the crawling cracks on stained glass.**

3 **Branched lightning** flamed in the **cacophonous,** autumn sky. It fizzed with its **fulvous-gold** ardour. The **radiant lightning** was **as vitrified as the creeping ice-cracks on a frozen pond.**

4 **Contorted lightning** flared under the **churning,** autumn sky. It **fizzled** with **gamboge-gold** streaks. The **resplendent lightning** was shaped **like crippled capillaries.**

5 **Crooked lightning** flashed under the **crumpling,** autumn sky. It **hissed** its **gaslight-gold** hatred. The **scintillating lightning** was **like electrified frizzy hair.**

6 **Dendriform-shaped lightning** slashed through the **moiling** sky. It **scorched** through it with its **glitter-gold** lasers. The **alien lightning** was **like misshapen plasma-streams.**

7 **Forked lightning** streaked across the **roiling** sky. It **seared** through it with its **globe-gold** wrath. The **arcane lightning** was **like the ruinous cracks on crumbling mortar.**

8 **Pronged lightning** wriggled in the **schizophrenic sky.** It **sizzled** through it with its **God-goldened** glory. The **otherworldly lightning** was shaped like **spread-eagled solar-rivers.**

9 **Splayed lightning** writhed in the **thunderous,** autumn sky. It **skewered** through it with its **halo-gold** spreading branches. The **sorcerous lightning** was shaped **like twisted limbs.**

10 **Veined lightning** zigzagged through the **weeping** sky. It **zoomed** to earth with its **star blaze-gold** branches. The **unearthly lightning** was shaped **like a witch's, warped whip.**

LEVEL 5: COMPLEX WRITING: SAMPLE PARAGRAPH

I ran towards the mighty oak, the only shelter in the field. Above me, something strange was happening. The nitrous-blue sky of a moment ago was morphing into something much more sinister. The clouds began to churn. Boiling and roiling like a vortex of hatred, they paused, coalesced and finally fused into a vast thundercloud of pagan-black. The land became tomb-still. The vaporous water-fountain loomed ominously overhead. A shroud of eerie silence descended. Nothing moved. Nothing stirred. Nothing dared to breathe. All at once, the first splatters of rain fell and the sound of a sonic boom rent the hushed peace. Thunder rumbled, a clangorous clap of fury like heavens anvil being rung with rage. A sudden flash seemed to stun the cracked sky. A gash of liquid light appeared from the breach above, a lesion in its seething surface. The sky still steamed like a witch's cauldron as pronged lightning spit and hissed like sizzling pulsar-whips. It looked like an upturned version of Neptune's fiery fork. An electrostatic crackling, natures nylon-shock, charged the atmosphere. It buzzed, cackled and fizzed with furious intensity. Splayed tentacles of glitter-gold blasted forth. I desperately increased my pace, fearing that I would be zapped. An explosion of lightning-flame emblazoned the Stygian sky, scarring its darkness. It writhed in its fleeting agony before illuminating into sorcerous sheet-lightning. It skewered through the sky and a single vein arrowed towards the oak tree. It squeaked once in terror before rupturing, fracturing and finally splintering. With a resounding crack, the once-mighty oak fell into two pieces, its heart tasered out. The lightning's fury and scintillating brilliance spent, it flared once more, fizzled fatally and faded. It left behind a stricken oak tree and a grateful survivor.

LEVEL 5: COMPLEX WRITING: THE SILENCE OF THE LAMBS

The autumn sky was as bright as Zeus' eyes. Nary a cloud blemished its bliss-blue complexion and the sun was like a glowing medallion pinned to a sheet of white paper. I ambled through the meadow, enjoying its peaceful air and the way it seemed to stretch into eternity. The grass was fairyland-green and the gentle swish of the blades, swaying to and fro, was hypnotic. It was like autumn's dreamscape.

In the centre of this large vale, quite some distance away, was a wizened oak tree. Its gnarled and hoary girth lay under a tangled old man's beard of leaf and bough. In a far-away field, stilt-legged lambs gambolled and frolicked with each other in merry innocence. The mountains in the distance loomed into the sky with a heaven-kissing majesty, silent and stern. Nothing disturbed my peace. It was merely the oak and I, just like in the storybooks. The sweep of sky, the lack of sigh, made me feel like I was walking through the finespun masterstrokes of a Michelangelo painting. I decided to rest my weary head for a while and let the spiritual beauty of this Jerusalem of nature seep into me further. Resting my head on my knapsack, I drifted away into infinity, letting the locked-away memories of joyful times steal into my dreams. A drowsy smile played on my lips and I floated into slumberland.

When I woke up, the sky was as black as the devil's soul. The clouds were damnation-black and glared down balefully at me. Like a tightening noose, the sky seemed to be coiling in on itself, purring with a suppressed rage. A distant rumbling, much like the sound of an avalanche, echoed in the air. The world became cellar-dark and the buckling, heaving sky looked fit to collapse down on top of me. Then there was an explosion like a sonic boom and I feared for my safety. Doom-black clouds, pregnant with malice, churned and roiled. They looked as vaporous as mist and as fleecy as black wool.

Then the rain came. It wasn't the nectar-of-the-gods type rain beloved of all those wandering adventurers lost in the desert. It was icy, stinging nails of rain that seemed to strip my skin and shrink my soul. Then the hailstone came. They were bone-white and as big as baseballs. They bombarded me with their spite and I had to put my rucksack above my head. Hobson's choice was facing me. I could die on my knees out in the meadow or risk the lightning under the leafy womb of the oak tree. Mussolini's famous quote came to me unbidden as I pondered my options. "Better to live one day as a lion than a hundred years as a sheep". I decided to be a lion. I ran. It occurred to me as I ran that he might have retracted that one (just before they hung him and his mistress upside down from a girder in the Piazzale Loreto in Milan).

I made it to the oak tree just in time. A clanking sound could be heard from the sky. It was if a huge anvil was being dragged across the vault of heaven against its will. Branched lightning lit up the Stygian sky. They were like liquid, golden ore streaks that were being moulded and forged into forks above my head. Buzzing and hissing, they trembled with the anger of being shackled to the sky since time began. They say that there are no atheists on a storm-tossed ship. I had my Damascene moment also and I prayed to the Lord above. He mustn't have heard me over the awful thunderclaps and the fizzing sound of electricity in the air, nature's nylon-shock. A single vein of lightning, large and fearsome, blazed out in the sky. Writhing and wriggling with the pain of its existence, it flashed once, glossy and polished, like a cold, gold prong of the Apocalypse.

Then it hit the tree. Lightning is the megawatt smile of nature, but there was nothing friendly about the terrawatts of violence it unleashed. It hit the shaggy head of the tree with an explosion of branched lightning-flame that shook the old man to his core. He tottered, staggered and then had time to squeak once in terror before the lightning splintered him in two. With a mighty crash that shook the ground, he came apart like a split pear. Three hundred years from little acorn to mighty oak meant little to nature. Three hundred years of brooding silence, dripping memories and questing roots were paid for with his destruction. Three hundred years of survival only to see his heart tasered into oblivion.

My own heart wasn't doing too well either. My left ear was on the ground, my eyes looking at the world from an ant's point of view. Wreaths of steam were rising slowly from the oak, all that was left of its soul. I could smell the sweet, sickly smell of singed grass and the faint perfume of scorched clothes told me I was in trouble. The quote from Mussolini came to me again, and although I strained my ears to hear, all I could hear from the fields next door, before drifting away, was the silence of the lambs.

USING A DICTIONARY AND PSYCHOLOGY

Twenty years of teaching English to a wide range of ages, abilities and personalities has taught me one valuable lesson. **Very rarely does the product matter; it is the packaging that counts.** This means that bringing knowledge, pedagogical skills and energy to a classroom is sometimes not enough to guarantee a successful lesson. The one formula that always works is a reward system, however. It may be the remarkable power of praise. It may be the incalculable benefits of raising someone's brittle self-esteem. It may even be as simple as massaging an ego. Sometimes, however, even these fail. What does one do then?

The two rewards I find incredibly uplifting have a transformative effect on a child. They guarantee success every time. That is because they are tangible, immediate and separate the student from his peers. Deep down, every growing child and adolescent want to be acknowledged as unique. In a school environment where they can feel they are reduced to the lowest common denominator, they crave that extra bit of validation.

That is where pear drops and homework off come into the equation.

Every day, in every class, one pupil gets to win a pear drop. It has gone to the stage where I'm being offered bribes and the keys to Shangri-La if I could just rig the outcome. I kid you not. That is because the pear drop has become a symbol of excellence, a glistening pearl of perfection in a world gone mad. I very rarely give it out to the most educationally gifted, however. They win homework off if they get an 'A' in their assignment and they leave the class feeling vindicated for their brilliance. So who gets the pear drop?

The pear drop is normally reserved for the student who needs it most. I often wonder sometimes if, deep down, they don't realize what I'm doing. From my perspective, even when dealing with nineteen year old students, it doesn't seem as if they do. Occasionally, some lone student with highly developed emotional intelligence will suspect it, but that's as far as it goes. Meanwhile, I'm looking for the student with the crumpled face, the stricken look or an apathy that is not common to that student. I will ask a question I know that student can answer, all the hands will shoot up and, remarkably, I will ask him or her to answer. On the rare days that the entire class is lethargic or feeling the pressure of school, the whole class gets one. What does this have to do with a dictionary, you might ask? The answer is simple. **A method or system, any system, is only monotonous if the outcome is predictable**. Then it becomes mundane and self-defeating. That is particularly true of education.

The same rule may be applied to dictionary work. The dictionary must remain a constant but the methodology of its use does not have to be. A dictionary is the bible of English. There is no greater gift to a child than to encourage its use as the most important aspect of their development in an English context. **How** you achieve that is the trick. Underneath are some tips for its use.

1. It should always be accompanied by a 'New Vocabulary' notebook. If the ability of the student/s is low, two or three words a day to look up is sufficient. If they are operating at a very high level, ten words per day is the absolute maximum.

2. Every new word they look up in the dictionary should be written into the notebook with its definition. As part of the homework, they should be asked to learn off X amount of definitions commensurate with their ability. Either you as their educator, or their peers, should ask them to repeat the definition the next day.

3. It is a myth to think that extremely weak students cannot keep up with the class or their peers. Certainly, they will need more time. Grant it to them. I have had to reteach the alphabet to twelve year olds and I thought it was very rewarding to see them flourish once they had the tools to look up the dictionary. It is the number one method for realigning the neuro-linguistic processes of a weak student. The most important thing to remember about the Intelligence Quotient test is that it is not immutable. Students who test as geniuses may re-test as average or worse in later life. The opposite is also true for those with so-called 'chronically weak' test results but who can be encouraged to be lifelong learners. A zest for learning and the ability to adapt is the ninth intelligence and the most under rated.

4. After a certain amount of time, perhaps a month or less, the New Vocabulary notebook will reach 'saturation point'. This means that the student will start forgetting the words he/she originally learned. Don't let them! Encourage them to look back at the words every so often. Put aside a certain amount of time for this. Revision is next to Godliness in the land of the educator.

5. Read a story with challenging diction. Encourage them to stop you when a new word is encountered so that they can look up its meaning and write it down.

6. Encourage the dynamic of paired excellence. Give them a break from your voice and let them challenge each other by asking the questions you normally would.

7. Offer them a pear drop if they can find a word in the dictionary that you can't define. Welcome to their world. At the start it is humbling, but that will pass. You are teaching them and yourself a valuable lesson; nobody has a monopoly on knowledge, but empathy is a gift.

THE DARK FOREST

COLOUR

LEVEL 1	LEVEL 2	LEVEL 3	LEVEL 4	LEVEL 5	OTHERS
bile-brown	toxic-brown	mottled-brown	blotched-brown	phlegm-brown	
bladder-brown	nicotine-brown	malady-brown	brindled-brown	sputum-brown	

1. *Ghastly ferns* pockmarked the floor of the bile-brown forest.
2. *Gruesome toadstools* pitted the floor of the toxic-brown forest.
3. *Grotesque fungi* stained the floor of the mottled-brown forest.
4. *Ghoulish hummus* blemished the floor of the blotched-brown forest.
5. *Grisly spores* sprinkled the floor like gremlin-dust. They glittered as wickedly as the devil's pennies.

A MONSTERS FEAST

chewing and chomping trolls	gnawing and gnashing ogres	slurping and slobbering vampires	gurgling and guzzling hobgoblins	munching and masticating cannibals	
champing and crunching witches	gobbling and grinding dire wolves	smearing and salivating ghouls	dribbling and drivelling night walkers	quaffing and wallowing revenants	

1. The *hellish dire wolves* were champing and crunching on the bones.
2. The *malformed ogres* were gnawing and gnashing on the bones.
3. The *accursed vampires* were slurping on and slobbering over the blood.
4. The *hellacious hobgoblins* were gurgling and guzzling on the remains.
5. The *abominable cannibals* were munching and masticating on the crunchy bones.

DARK WOODS

shady glades	gloomy scrubs	sunless copses	dusky wealds	fuliginous holts	
shadowy groves	murky thickets	sooty coppices	turbid spinneys	lucifugous hursts	

1. *Combs of moss* hung in shady glades.
2. *Bristles of moss* swayed in murky thickets.
3. *Spikes of tough moss* trailed from the trees in sunless copses.
4. *Needles of prickly moss* swung uneasily from the dusky wealds.
5. *Daggers of sharp moss* dangled and brooded in the lucifugous hursts.

BAD AIR

stale air	musty air	dank air	clammy air	fusty air	
stuffy air	mouldy air	decaying air	claustrophobic	frowsty air	

1. *Wailing* sounds echoed through the stale air of the dark forest.
2. *Whooping* sounds rang through the mouldy air of the dark forest.
3. *Whimpering* sounds resounded through the dank air of the dark forest.
4. The dreadful sound of *weeping and gibbering* resonated in the clammy air.
5. The macabre sound of *ululating and moaning* reverberated through the fusty air.

YE OLDE FORESTE

ancestral	otherworldly	primeval	arcane	eldritch	
antiquated	unearthly	primordial	atavistic	preternatural	

1. *Pools of dark light* hung between the trees in the ancestral forest.
2. *Pockets of doom-black light* hung between the trees in the unearthly forest.
3. *Collars of chaos-black light* moved between the trees in the primeval forest.
4. *Reams of dire-black light* seemed to fill in the spaces in the arcane forest.
5. *Screens of damnation-black light* menaced the open spaces in the preternatural forest.

OTHER IMAGES

reaching and sprawling limbs of trees	thigh-thick creepers	deadly hellebore slurping the nutrients	stygian-black streams and syrup-slow	cobwebs shimmering like meshed steel	
trees glaring like silent sentries	oxblood-red toadstools	mottled bark like bubbling soup frozen in time	clouds of cannonball-black flies	pestilent steam like spooky incense	

1. Strange creatures *crept* under the reaching and sprawling limbs of trees.

2. Brutish animals *crawled* for food under the thigh-thick creepers.

3. Grim-faced reavers *padded* silently around the nutrient-slurping, deadly hellebore.

4. Fiendish monsters *prowled* around the stygian-black, syrup-slow streams.

5. The pestilent steam of the forest rose up like spooky incense as the night walkers *stalked* their prey.

FOREST POISONS

fool's parsley	cuckoo pint	larkspur	deadly nightshade	hellebore	
wolfs bane	cowbane	panther cap	devils bolete	hemlock	

1. The flowers around the fool's parsley were all ***hanging weakly***.

2. The flowers around the cuckoo pint were all ***drooping***.

3. The last surviving flower in the bed of panther cap was ***flagging***.

4. A single flower survived next to the deadly nightshade. It was ***sickly and sagging***.

5. A lone flower withered next to the hemlock. It was ***palsied and wilting***.

SMELL

musty smell	acrid odour	rank miasma	toxic reek	rancid	

				effluvium	
yucky pong	fetid stench	pungent tang	tart emanation	mephitic nip	

1. The musty smells of the forest *leaked* up to the inky shadows between the trees.
2. The fetid stench of the forest *trickled* up to the ebony shadows between the trees.
3. The rank miasma *oozed* up to the curtains of corruption-black between the trees.
4. The toxic reek *drizzled* up to the sacrilege-black shrouds of shadow.
5. The mephitic nip of the forest *seeped* up to the desolation-black drapes of shadow.

SENSATION

hair-raising	teeth-gritting	blood-churning	marrow-congealing	mind-numbing	
spine-chilling	throat-constricting	vein-freezing	pulse-quickening	nightmare-inspiring	

1. The *blunt clubs* the cannibals carried were spine-chilling.
2. The *stout cudgels* the cannibals raised in the air were throat-constricting.
3. The *crushing bludgeons* the cannibals flourished were blood-churning.
4. The cannibals wielded their *fiendish knobkerries* and it was marrow-congealing.
5. The cannibals brandished their *diabolic shillelaghs* and it was nightmare-inspiring.

THE TASTE OF BLOOD

oily taste	sour taste	sickening taste	acidic taste	acerbic taste	
fishy taste	metallic taste	vampirish taste	caustic taste	astringent taste	

1. The oily taste of our own blood was *sickening*.
2. The sour taste of our own blood was *nauseating*.
3. The vampirish taste of our own blood was *vomit-inducing*.
4. The acidic taste of our own blood was *macabre and stomach-churning*.
5. The astringent taste of our own blood was akin to *gall and wormwood*.

LEVEL 1: BASIC SENTENCES

1. The trees in the forest were **bladder-brown. COLOUR**
2. The trolls were **chewing and chomping** on red meat. **A MONSTERS FEAST**
3. They ate under the **shadowy groves. DARK WOODS**
4. The air was **stuffy. BAD AIR**
5. The forest was **old and antiquated. YE OLDE FORESTE**
6. The trees were staring at me like **silent sentries. OTHER IMAGES**
7. I crept around the poisonous **wolfs bane. FOREST POISONS**
8. There was a **yucky pong** in the forest. **SMELL**
9. It was a **hair-raising** place. **SENSATION**
10. I injured my mouth. The **fishy** taste of blood was disgusting.

LEVEL 2: A BASIC PARAGRAPH

The trees in the dark forest were **nicotine-brown**. Orcs were **gobbling meat and grinding** on bone. **Gloomy scrubs** hid dangerous creatures. The **musty air** was difficult to breathe. The forest was old and **otherworldly**. **Oxblood-red toadstools** littered the ground. **Poisonous cowbane** grew next to them. An **acrid odour** hung off everything. It was a **teeth-gritting** experience. I bit my tongue with nervousness and the **metallic taste** of blood filled my mouth.

LEVEL 3: CREATIVE PARAGRAPHS

The trees in the forest were **malady-brown**. Grains of poison begrimed the bark and gleamed like witch dust. Trolls haunted the **sooty coppices**, salivating over their prey and **smearing** the blood over their heavy faces. The **decaying air** and stifling atmosphere provided the perfect abode for those who worshipped the darkness rather than the light. In the dense shadows, spiders clutched their snare-strings. Their webs shimmered like meshed steel dipped in silver. Eyes a-flame with hunger, they were hoping to dine on bloated bodies and slurp on hot blood.

The forest was **primordial**. Centuries-old trees with sprawling limbs guarded the darkness, blotting out any sunlight. Their bark was mottled and splotched, as if **bubbled soup had been frozen in time** on its surface. Clumpy combs of wet moss dangled from their rotten boughs. Underneath the moss, **lethal larkspur** peppered the mulchy floor. A **pungent tang** oozed from every sentient being in the forest. Bewailing sounds ghosted through the trees.

Whether it was from victim or victor, only the forest could tell. It was truly a place to make your **veins freeze** over. Everything considered edible in another forest was nauseating here. It left you with the same, **sickening taste** of your own blood. It was a forest to be avoided.

LEVELS 4 AND 5: COMPLEX WRITING
The Dark Forest: Womb of Pandemonium
Transylvania- circa 1350
"Cannibals always feast under a blood-red moon."

Every child in his village had laughed at the forest-lore passed down by the woodcutters all those years ago. Now the villagers themselves were gone, swept away as if by some invisible hand, and he knew the saying to be true. Looking at the Godless scene unfolding in front of him, the king's monster hunter believed he would die here today. He was duty bound to help, but there were too many of the heathens to fight. Their spice-blue eyes and waxy skin pallor marked them out as flesh-eaters. He watched, spellbound and revolted in equal measure, as they danced a ghastly ritual around a huge fire, ululating to the beat of a rumbling drum. Their limbs were akimbo and their expressions frenzied as they dragged the first victim towards the pig-spit. Mounds of old, gnawed bone, a midden heap of gleaming ribs and grinning skulls, caught the fires blaze and sickened him. His flesh crept and the hair on his neck rose like the hackles of a dog. Fear, a feeling he was unused to, felt like melting tallow under the surface of his skin, feverish and hot. The sanguine-red moon flooded the holt, giving off an unearthly glow of flame and fire.

The vast, contorted tree he leaned against leaked its sticky sap like the poisoned back of a toad, burning his hand. He snatched it away. He was at the outermost edge of the fires glow, concealed in the murky shadow of the tree's massive vines. They twisted up insanely, like the despairing limbs of the damned begging for forgiveness. Above him, ghostly horsetails of moss were hanging from barrel-thick boughs like a poltergeist's entrails. A large pearl of rain gathered at the bottom of one of these spectre-strings. It alone had made its way through the labyrinthine canopy of hoary limbs and leafy bowers. It teetered there for an age. Then with a slimy pop it released itself. A solitary moonbeam speared through the trees at that moment. The globule glowed red, like the vile drop of a blood oath, before splashing onto the rotten humus. The wraithy horsetails shivered once with a swished whisper of hatred and settled back into their silent spite. The hoary tree knots glared at him like baleful eyes. He felt like the forest was infecting him with its alien pox.

Never had he encountered these emotions on his many hunts. He had quarried after dread vampyres in the fathomless bowels and dripping basins of the deepest caves. He had ascended sky-kissing mountains to seek out blood-besmeared trolls. He had even, as a favour to a foreign king, crossed a tyranny of distance to bring to bay the Black Golwroth of Karaganda in his lair. But this dark forest was different to anywhere he had been before. Hunting after base beasts into dens and burrows, down begrimed pits and through gloomy hollows, could not begin to compare to this gullet of madness. Just being here felt like partaking in an unholy parody of life. He tried to think of a word for the renders of human flesh he was gazing upon, but it eluded him. They had maggoted their way to this glade, burrowing like wood-weevils into the corrupted heart of the forest. He noted with contempt their filed-down fangs and brutish weapons; clunky clubs, brutal bull-axes and wicked sickles. It seemed fitting to him that they would inhabit this sacrilegious wood.

Two weeks of plunging through stunted coppices and hacking at misshapen thickets had gotten him here. It was a grotesque haunt, offensive to eye, ear and nostril. The air was hot and stale, burning his lungs like the fumes from brimstone. The floor of the forest belched up constant waves of foul and rancid odours that smelt like sickly excrement. All the freewheeling flotsam of the trees gathered there in blasted mounds of steaming mulch. The scorch of the sun didn't cause this. Only an occasional, listless ligament of light would pin-prick through the dense foliage. It was like a constipated beam of hopelessness, limply flickering. It had all the cheerless comfort of a dying candle flame. Heat was provided by the thickness of the forests canopy. It compressed down upon the lucifugous heads of those below, creating a sunless curtain of chaos-black. Toxic-yellow fungi tossed their pestilent spores into this goulash of decay. Deformed trees pressed in from the sides, adding to the mood of stuffy claustrophobia.

Only one trickling streamlet gasped its way through the stomach-souring compost. Like the river of hell, it was Acheron-black and gleamed with a deadly lustre. At its swirling edges, bladder-brown leaves got sucked into the inky morass and added to the treacly pollution. On the trees, wet clumps of glistening Jews Ear hinged themselves slickly to the bark like clotted pus. Their glossy texture resembled the skin of slugs. Over the bitter water, great screens of milky mist were heaving with their own steaming malice. Stealthy scarves of the mist detached themselves, slowly glided in silence and coiled serpent-like around helpless limbs.

Between the trees, wispy cobwebs threaded out like fibrous star-streak. They would be the sinewy tentacles of destruction for all those who would dare their tensile strength. Exhaling miasmas of rotting vapour rose up to meet the webs, while above, fevered eyes, glazed with hunger, waited among the endless damp. Cruel as those eyes were, they lacked the ferocity of the hunter's eyes.

Those eyes were scanning the shroud of shadow at the other side of the fire. There appeared to be a crude, stone building made of poorly built, bulging stone. It was lichen-encrusted and a rotting roof lay upon it. From its interior came the most piteous moans and stomach-souring thumps. A caterwauling sound, somewhere between a tortured whine and a despairing screech, echoed in the night air. The tormented screams of the victims seared his soul. He was kinless and kith-less, with neither family nor friend, yet he had been smelted in the fiery forge of violence since he was a child. He was no longer afraid. The blood-lust was upon him, a familiar feeling. He kissed his crucifix and left it to hang in the tree. Wrapped around each forearm were cords of thin rope, edged with serrated, razor-steel. He unfolded these, letting them hang from each hand. He had a sword and three throwing knives, but he left them in their sheaths. It would be gory work tonight, silent and bloody. He eased away from the tree, a foe far more deadly than the hemlock and wolfs bane his moccasins stepped over.

Skirting the glade, he made his way to the stone building. He couldn't see anyone guarding it, but could make out some horrible, stony voices from within. Their low harshness reminded him of lonely cemetery vaults and mildewed tombs. They were deep and seeped with malice. Creeping over to the wall, he searched for a gap between the stone to look through.
Four brutes with pop eyes and saucy beards stood over the villagers. They were wielding crude, bone-edged clubs. One of the bug-eyed heathens raised his club to continue his grisly work, but the monster-hunter had seen enough. "Abominations", he whispered. He prepared himself to meet his Creator in this womb of pandemonium. He crept up to the entrance and stepped in.....

SPELLINGS

The most noticeable effect of the electronic age, education wise, is the impact it has had on spellings and concentration levels. I have mentioned how a student may feel that he/she is the lowest common denominator (L.C.D) when he is in a school environment. The English language must feel the same way when confronted by the minimalist spelling approach favoured by text messaging, twitter, Facebook and e-mailing. My term for it is 'L.C.D syndrome' because it reduces English to a bunch of phonics, phonemes and syllables that can take away from the beauty, scope and power of the language. If indeed we are all shackled by the limits of our imagination, and by definition, our language, it is the educator's job to reaffirm the grounding and base that every child needs to succeed.

Students have a valid argument when arguing that spelling words correctly is a disadvantage in these mediums. I would tend to agree with them on that. The counter argument, however, is that **misspelling should be a choice, not a trend**. They will encounter plenty of mediums in their life where spellings will be crucial to leaving a good impression of their educational attainment. That is why there is a spelling worksheet attached to the book. The value of good spellings can never be underestimated. At all times, a student should be praised for **attempting** to spell. Progress varies among them from tortuous to exceptional. It is the effort that is important sometimes, not the end result. At the start of the school year, I put one word on the board for the incoming first years. I ask them to take it home and learn it off. It is:

Pneumonoultramicroscopicsilicovolcanoconiosis

Ironically, its nickname is P45. There are 45 letters and 19 syllables in this word. I break it down into its parts after the gasps of astonishment have died down. It then looks like this:

Pneumono/ ultra/ micro/ scopic/ silico/ volcano/ coniosis

The word immediately becomes more accessible. We then spend 20 minutes chanting it to get a feel for it. While we are chanting, we are looking at its spelling on the blackboard. I will then rub out the board and ask them to spell it as I call it out. I have taught many children who can spell it from memory before the 40 minute class is over. Usually, about half the class will have it learned to perfection by the next day. That is because it comes with a reward exclusive to their class; homework off for a week. The sense of pride and achievement that accrues from it is worth the effort. The point is that, in my experience, there's no excuse for poor spelling. There is poor ability, poor motivation and poor instruction; but there's no excuse for poor spelling.

DESCRIBING FEMALES

FIGURE

LEVEL 1	LEVEL 2	LEVEL 3	LEVEL 4	LEVEL 5	OTHERS
an hour glass figure	a sculpted figure	a comely figure	a queenly figure	a mermaid's figure	
shapely figure	a svelte figure	a curvaceous figure	an Amazonian figure	a willowy figure	

1. She had a *slim*, hourglass figure.
2. She had a *slender*, svelte figure.
3. She had a *supple*, curvaceous figure.
4. She had a *willowy*, queenly figure.
5. She had a gymslip-thin, *statuesque* figure.

BODY

elf-thin	whip-thin	stem-thin	wafer-thin	orphan-thin	
imp-thin	twine-thin	sapling-thin	waif-thin	mannequin-thin	

1. She was elf-thin and her *lips were ripe*.
2. She was whip-thin and her *lips were juicy*.
3. She was sapling-thin and her *lips were lush*.
4. She was waif-thin and her *lips were luscious*.
5. She was orphan-thin and her *lips were ravishing*.

WAIST

a bumblebee	a tapered	a chalice	a goblet	an oxbow	

waist	waist	shaped waist	shaped waist	waist	
wasp-waisted	sylph-like waist	a curvilinear waist	a decanter shaped waist	a yew bow waist	

1. She had a bumblebee waist and **berry-red lips**.
2. She had a sylph-like waist and **raspberry-red lips**.
3. She had a chalice shaped waist and **strawberry-red lips**.
4. Her waist was goblet shaped and she had she had **cherry-red lips**.
5. Her waist was oxbow shaped and she had **fuchsia-red lips**.

COMPLEXION

glowing skin	a bronzed complexion	a citron tint	an apricot hue	a pigment perfect tincture	
glossy skin	a burnished complexion	a saffron tint	an ochrous hue	a peaches and cream tincture	

1. Her skin was **perfect** and glowing
2. She had a **flawless**, bronzed complexion.
3. It had a **peerless**, citron tint to it.
4. She had **impeccable** skin with an ochrous hue.
5. She had **unblemished** skin with a peaches and cream complexion.

EYEBROWS

slender eyebrows	arched eyebrows	crescent shaped eyebrows	pencil-thin eyebrows	quarter-moon eyebrows	
plucked eyebrows	curved eyebrows	eclipse shaped eyebrows	symmetrical eyebrows	sliver-of-moon eyebrows	

1. She had plucked eyebrows of **midnight-black**.

2. She had arched eyebrows of *raven-black*.

3. She had eclipse shaped eyebrows of *coral-black*.

4. She had *mamba-black*, symmetrical eyebrows.

5. She had *kohl-black,* sliver-of-moon eyebrows.

EYELASHES

silky	sweeping	languid	beetle's-leg	Cleopatra	
velvety	fine-spun	languorous	spider's-leg	Merovingian	

1. Her eyelashes were silky over her *acorn shaped eyes*.

2. She had finespun eyelashes over her *hazelnut shaped eyes*.

3. She had languorous eyelashes of feather-black atop her *walnut shaped eyes*.

4. She had spider's-leg eyelashes that fluttered over her *grape shaped eyes*.

5. She had Cleopatra eyelashes of a lush, succubus-black over her *ungulate shaped eyes*.

EARS

elfin ears	delicate ears	scrolled ears	a cherub's ears	seashell shaped ears	
sea nymph ears	ethereal ears	whorled ears	a seraph's ears	scallop shaped ears	

1. She had elfin ears and *half-moon cheekbones*.

2. She had ethereal ears and *domed cheekbones*.

3. They were whorled like a sea nymph's over her *prominent cheekbones*.

4. She had the fragile ears of a cherub over her *pinched-in cheekbones*.

5. She had gimcrack, seashell shaped ears and *concave cheekbones*.

NOSE

a pointy nose	a button nose	an elegant nose	a pixie's nose	a Muses' nose	
a dainty nose	a pert nose	a linear nose	a film star's nose	a diva's nose	

1. She had a pointy nose and **blush-pink** lips.
2. She had a pert nose and **blossom-pink** lips.
3. She had a linear nose and **sorbet-pink** lips.
4. She had a film star's nose above her **orchid-pink** lips.
5. She had a diva's nose perched atop her **blushing, pilgrim-pink** lips.

TEETH

shining, halo-white teeth.	dazzling, angel-white teeth.	pristine, calcite-white teeth.	bewitching, unicorn-white teeth.	fluorescent, porcelain-white teeth.	
gleaming, bleach-white teeth.	sparkling, archangel-white teeth.	luminous, heavenly-white teeth.	beguiling, oyster-white teeth.	spellbinding, wizard-white teeth.	

1. She had gleaming, bleach-white teeth and a **cherubic smile**.
2. She had sparkling, archangel-white teeth and an **angelic smile**.
3. She had pristine, calcite-white teeth and an **electrifying smile**.
4. She had bewitching, unicorn-white teeth and a **megastar** smile.
5. She had spellbinding, wizard-white teeth and a **megawatt** smile.

FINGERNAILS

varnished fingernails	siren-red fingernails	film star fingernails	Venus-red fingernails	pendant shaped	
manicured fingernails	carmine-red fingernails	hennaed fingernails	Aphrodite-red	stiletto shaped	

1. She had manicured fingernails and a **dimpled chin**.
2. She had siren-red fingernails and a **hazel shell chin**.
3. She had hennaed fingernails and a **gently cleft chin**.
4. She had Aphrodite-red fingernails and an **acorn cup chin**.
5. She had stiletto shaped fingernails and a **coracle-perfect chin**.

CREATIVITY

'Thoughts that glow and words that flow'. That is a mantra that every creative writing class should adopt. It distils the purpose of descriptive writing down to its very essence. The key question surrounding creativity is whether it is inbuilt or whether it can be taught. The answer is that both are applicable. There are people who claim to have the ability to 'taste' colours and apply colours to different sounds. This is called **synaesthesia**. Among others, Billy Joel and Eddie van Halen have this gift. Marilyn Monroe had it and Stevie Wonder has it also. I would argue that everyone has a residue of this type of 'feel' for individual words, sounds and colours in them.

A fascinating sub plot to this is Tolkien's claim in 1955, backed up by tens of thousands since, as to what was the most beautiful word in the English language. Edgar Allen Poe wrote a poem based on its syllables and hundreds of writers have backed up Tolkien's claim. The answer is on page 200. Also included is a list of 100 'pulse' words. That is my term for a word that can be beautiful, impactful or have a powerful effect on a passage of writing.

In recent times, it has become fashionable to apply the suffix 'scape' at the end of a noun to paint an image of scope and vastness. Underneath are some examples. There is also a sample of words using 'dust'. The words 'sprinkling stardust' have more wonder, beauty and resonance than any others I know besides 'sole heir' and 'cheque enclosed'! The last column is a list of pulse words that can improve any story.

The 'scape' suffix	Words with dust	Pulse words
cloudscape	doom dust	lush
dreamscape	dream dust	mouth watering
moonscape	fairy dust	glamour
seascape	gremlin dust	sizzling
skyscape	imp dust	vermilion
smellscape	pixie dust	sorcery
snowscape	moon dust	fragrance
treescape	stardust	glimmering
waterscape	witch dust	magnetism
winterscape	wizard dust	angelic

DESCRIBING FEMALES

RED HAIR

LEVEL 1	LEVEL 2	LEVEL 3	LEVEL 4	LEVEL 5	OTHERS
mercury-red hair	magma-red hair	ruby-red hair	solferino-red hair	vermeil-red hair	
molten-red hair	lava-red hair	rouge-red hair	Titian-red hair	vermilion-red hair	

1. Her hair was mercury-red and it **tumbled** over her shoulders.
2. Her hair was magma-red and it **crashed** over her shoulders.
3. Her hair was rouge-red and it **spiralled** over her shoulders.
4. She had tresses of Titian-red and they **plummeted** over her shoulders.
5. She had swirls of vermilion-red and they **cascaded** over her shoulders.

BLACK HAIR

midnight-black hair	kohl-black hair	coral-black hair	sable-black hair	vulcanite-black hair	
ebony-black hair	moon shadow-black hair	cobalt-black hair	maw-black hair	obsidian-black hair	

1. Her hair was midnight-black and it **flowed** over her shoulders.
2. Her hair was kohl-black and it **plunged** over her shoulders.
3. Her hair was coral-black and it **toppled** over her shoulders.
4. She had locks of sable-black and they **surged** over her shoulders.
5. She had tresses of obsidian-black and they **swooped** over her shoulders.

BLONDE HAIR

sunrise-gold hair	moon gleam-gold hair	star flame-gold hair	ore-gold hair	Arc-of-Covenant	

				gold hair	
sunset-gold	moon glint-gold hair	star beam-gold hair	harp string-gold hair	Valkyrie-gold hair	

1. She had *lush*, sunrise-gold hair.
2. She had *lavish*, moon gleam-gold hair.
3. She had *luscious*, star flame-gold hair.
4. Her hair was ore-gold bright and *luxurious*.
5. Her hair was Arc-of-Covenant gold and *luxuriant*.

BROWN HAIR

locks of chestnut-brown hair	wisps of auburn-brown	tumbles of russet-brown	swirls of caramel-brown hair	skeins of copper-brown hair	
coils of leaf-brown hair	ringlets of tawny-brown hair	tresses of mousy-brown hair	spools of nougat-brown hair	Restoration curls of cinnamon-brown hair	

1. Locks of chestnut-brown hair *curtained* her oval face.
2. Ringlets of tawny-brown hair *veiled* her heart shaped face.
3. Tresses of russet-brown hair *shrouded* her Slavic face.
4. Swirls of caramel-brown hair *wreathed* her moon shaped face.
5. Restoration curls of cinnamon-brown hair *garlanded* her angular face.

COLOUR OF EYES

dreamy, bliss-blue eyes	alluring, galaxy-blue eyes	lambent, jade-green eyes	dewy, mist valley-green eyes	effervescent, champagne-brown eyes	
languorous, rapture-blue eyes	enticing, constellation-blue eyes	fulgent, beryl-green eyes	nebulous, Eden-green eyes	vivacious, virility-brown eyes	

1. She had dreamy, bliss-blue eyes. They were **globe round**.
2. She had alluring, galaxy-blue eyes. They were **orbit round**.
3. She had lambent, jade-green eyes. They were **pond round**.
4. She had dewy, mist valley-green eyes. They were **duck-pond round**.
5. She had effervescent, champagne-brown eyes. They were **dew-pond round**.

LIPS

puffy lips	bee stung lips	oxbow lips	trout pout lips	silicone enhanced lips	
pouting lips	heart shaped lips	Cupid's bow lips	botox boosted	collagen enhanced lips	

1. She had puffy lips. They were **kiss-inspiring and satin soft**.
2. She had bee-stung lips. They were **sugar plum sweet and silk soft**.
3. She had Cupid's bow lips. They were **plummy, plump and suede soft**.
4. She had trout pout lips. They were **succulent, sultry and velvet soft**.
5. She had silicone enhanced lips. They were **sumptuous, sensuous and velour soft**.

SWEET LIPS

honey sweet lips	strawberry sweet lips	sugar sweet lips	cherry sweet lips	nectar sweet lips	
syrup sweet lips	saccharine sweet lips	sugar candy sweet lips	melon sweet lips	sherbet sweet lips	

1. She had honey sweet lips. They were **lilac soft**.
2. She had saccharine sweet lips. They were **blossom soft**.
3. She had sugar sweet lips. They were **butter soft**.
4. She had cherry sweet lips. They were **beeswax soft**.
5. She had sherbet sweet lips. They were **pillow soft**.

PERSONALITY

a cheerful personality	a bubbly personality	an elegant personality	a demure personality	a winning personality	

a joyous personality	a bouncy personality	a ladylike personality	a genteel personality	an infectious personality	

1. She had a cheerful **character**.
2. She had a bubbly **outlook**.
3. She had a ladylike **temperament**.
4. She had a genteel **persona**.
5. She had a winning **disposition**.

A SWEET VOICE

a soothing voice	a sugary voice	a nectarine voice	a dulcet voice	a melodious voice	
a songbird sweet voice	a syrup sweet voice	a saccharine voice	a dulcimer sweet voice	a mellifluous voice	

1. She had a songbird sweet voice and her hair *blazed* in the sun.
2. She had a syrup sweet voice and her hair *flashed* in the sun.
3. She had a nectarine voice and her hair *glinted* in the sun.
4. She had a dulcimer sweet voice and her hair *gleamed* in the sun's rays.
5. She had a melodious voice and her opulent hair *glittered* in the beams of the sun.

CLOTHES

grungy	vibrant	chic	voguish	cosmopolitan	
gothic	kidult	retro	fluoro	naff	

1. She wore gothic clothes in a **rebellious** way.
2. She wore kidult clothes in an **offbeat** way.
3. She wore chic, shredded clothes in a **mutinous** way.
4. She wore fluoro clothes in a **non-conforming** way.
5. She wore bleached, naff clothes in an **out of kilter** fashion.

LEVEL 1: BASIC SENTENCES

1. She had a **shapely** figure. **FIGURE**
2. It was **imp-thin**. **BODY**
3. She was **wasp-waisted**. **WAIST**
4. She had **glossy** skin. **COMPLEXION**
5. She had **slender** eyebrows. **EYEBROWS**
6. Her eyelashes were **velvety**. **EYELASHES**
7. She had **sea-nymph** ears. **EARS**
8. She had a **dainty** nose. **NOSE**
9. She had **shiny, halo-white** teeth. **TEETH**
10. Her fingernails were **varnished**. **FINGERNAILS**
11. Her hair was **molten-red**. **RED HAIR**
12. Her hair was **ebony-black**. **BLACK HAIR**
13. Her hair was **sunrise-gold**. **GOLD HAIR**
14. She had coils of **leaf-brown** hair. **BROWN HAIR**
15. She had **rapture-blue** eyes. **BLUE EYES**
16. She had **pouting** lips. **SHAPE OF LIPS**
17. She had **syrup-sweet** lips. **SWEET LIPS**
18. She had a **joyous** personality. **PERSONALITY**
19. She had a **soothing** voice. **SWEET VOICE**
20. She wore **grungy** clothes. **CLOTHES**

LEVEL 2: A BASIC PARAGRAPH

She had a **sculpted figure** which was **twine-thin**. Her **waist was tapered** and she had a **burnished complexion**. A pair of **arched eyebrows** looked down on **sweeping eyelashes**. Her **delicate ears** framed a **button nose**. A set of **dazzling, angel-white teeth** gleamed as she blew gently on her **carmine-red fingernails**. It was a pleasure to see her flowing, **moon shadow-black hair**. Her enticing, **constellation-blue eyes** gazed at me over her puffy, **heart shaped lips**. Her lips tasted **strawberry sweet** when I kissed her. She had a **bouncy personality** and a **sugary voice**, which I adored. Not content to be just another drone, she wore **vibrant clothes**.

LEVEL 3: CREATIVE PARAGRAPHS

I first met her on a holiday to an exotic country. The moons delicate light had just turned the world a-flame with silver when I saw her. She had a **comely figure** which was **stem-thin**. Her **curvilinear waist** didn't surprise me as much as the **saffron tint** to her complexion. She must be a native, I thought to myself. Her **crescent shaped eyebrows** inclined slightly as she saw me staring at her. I yelped at being caught. Her **languid eyelashes** of velvet-black blinked once slowly, as if to invite me over.

When I came closer, I noticed her **scrolled ears** and her **elegant nose**. She nuzzled me with her nose and I couldn't believe it. It was the custom for her people, I reckoned. It was love at first light. Her luminous, **heavenly-white teeth** flashed as she pawed at me with her **film star nails**. Her hair was a glorious **tumble of star beam-gold** and her **virility-brown eyes** set my heart a-thump. Her **oxbow lips** positively drooled with goodness. Oh! Those **sugar candy-sweet lips**, her **elegant personality**, all mesmerized me. She may not have had a **saccharine voice** or **retro clothes**, but what do you expect when two Labrador pups meet in a dog pound?

LEVEL 4: ADVANCED PARAGRAPHS

Her **Amazonian figure** sat well on her **wafer-thin body**. She had a **decanter shaped waist** and her complexion had an impeccable, **ochrous hue**. Her **pencil-thin eyebrows** eased down gently to her black, **beetle's-leg eyelashes**. A sculptor could not have fashioned her **seraph's ears** and **pixie's nose** any better.

When she broke into a smile, her beguiling, **oyster-white teeth** lit up the room. It could jolt you like an electric current when that **megawatt smile** gave you her full attention. Filed to perfection, her **Venus-red fingernails** ran through her **nougat-brown hair**. Spools of it plunged around her photogenic face and hid **a swan's neck**, elegant and smooth. I loved her nebulous, **Eden-green eyes** which were a-sparkle with the 'joie de vivre'. They were like two beryl-green jewels melted onto snow.

Her **calamine-pink lips** tasted like rose petals. It surprised me that they were plump and **botox-boosted** as she had a **demure**, timorous personality. She whispered to me in **a dulcet voice** as sweet as any songbird. Her **voguish clothes** still kept captive an aroma redolent of cinnamon and **meadow-fresh mint**. It lingered in the room long after she had gone.

LEVEL 5: COMPLEX WRITING: BEWARE THE BEAUTY

Her hair was **as emollient as eiderdown** and was like **a loom of molten-gold**. It swooped past her **ethereal neck**, framing her **Slavic face** perfectly. She looked at me with her **lemur-round eyes**. They were seductive and **rhapsody-blue**. My heart nearly stopped when she gazed at me. Her eyes were **like two plasma-blue gems slumbering in milky pools**. They were **a-smoulder with passion** and had a hypnotic quality to them. They were gleaming with an unearthly quality above her **concave cheekbones** and they shone with the faraway look of a star gazer.

Her **sliver-of-moon eyebrows** were burglar-black and stole my soul. If she had just batted those long and **languourous** eyelashes in my direction, I could have talked to her. I stared at her pouting, **silicone-enhanced** lips. They were **Aphrodite-red** and looked as sweet as strawberries. She had a telegenic look and a **statuesque figure**. It was comely to the eye and svelte and sultry. Her **sea-nymph ears**, tucked away in the glorious tresses of her hair, looked delicate and pared to perfection.

Her smile seemed fixed with fluorescent, **archangel-white teeth**. It was made more ravishing by her **uber-tan**. The summer sun had leaked in and burnished her bronze with its rays. I had heard that her voice was **as lilting and fluty as a nightingale**, but she never got the chance to talk to me. I didn't want to stare at her anymore as she carried herself in a **ladylike** and genteel manner. Her **cosmopolitan clothes** merely enforced my opinion of her. She was a gimlet-eyed paragon of pulchritude. What was the lesson I learned from that day? Never mix business with pleasure when you're dressing a mannequin!

SYNTAX

Syntax is the way that sentences are constructed. The golden rule in writing is: KISS. This means Keep It Simple, Silly. That is the phrase I use the most with my students. It means that sentences should not be overly lengthy, convoluted or burdensome to the eye. Unfortunately, I broke this rule deliberately many times in the construction of this book! That's because of the way the book is designed in a one-size-fits-all format. In some sentences, it was necessary to put in an extra word so that a fuller lexicon and variety of diction was available to the book's readers. A typical example of this was in the 'eyelashes' section of Describing Females. The sentences underneath the grid are below.

1. Her eyelashes were silky over her acorn shaped eyes.
2. She had finespun eyelashes over her hazelnut shaped eyes.
3. She had languorous eyelashes **of feather-black** atop her walnut shaped eyes.
4. She had spider's-leg eyelashes that fluttered over her grape shaped eyes.
5. She had Cleopatra eyelashes **of a lush, succubus-black** over her ungulate shaped eyes.

There is a syntactical problem with sentences three and five. It would be preferable to omit the words highlighted in bold. That would make the sentences less entangled and provide two images instead of three. The sentences would then look more presentable.

3. She had languorous eyelashes atop her walnut shaped eyes.
5. She had Cleopatra eyelashes over her ungulate shaped eyes.

A more pressing problem is the way in which text messaging has resulted in a form of pidgin English seeping into the work of students. It is no longer uncommon to be presented with a sentence that looks like this;

Wots up I said he said dat he was gud".

The only solution to this is to apply the same processes as this book does in order to stop the slaughter of our beautiful language! Rules of grammar and syntax should be constantly taught in order to give the students a wide base of knowledge from which to operate. Time and patience, allied to empathy about the challenges students face in the modern electronic world is required. Then sentences like the one below become commonplace.

"Are you well," I enquired? "I'm in good spirits," he responded.

DESCRIBING MALES

BLOND HAIR

LEVEL 1	LEVEL 2	LEVEL 3	LEVEL 4	LEVEL 5	OTHERS
Viking-gold hair	Nordic-gold hair	Aryan-gold hair	lions mane-gold hair	Achilles-gold hair	
Hercules-gold hair	Scandinavian-gold hair	Teutonic-gold hair	mother lode-gold hair	Apollo-gold hair	

1. He had *wavy*, Hercules-gold hair.
2. He had *mussed*, Nordic-gold hair.
3. He had *twirling*, Aryan-gold hair.
4. He had a *swirling*, lion's mane of gold hair.
5. He had *whisked*, Apollo-gold hair that danced in the wind.

SHORT HAIR

a crew cut	a Mohican hair cut	a marine haircut	a razor's-edge cur	a bald pate	
close cropped hair	a rooster cut	a military hair cut	a buzz-cut	a chrome dome	

1. He had a crew cut and *darting* eyes.
2. He had a rooster cut and *piercing* eyes.
3. He had a marine cut and *penetrating* eyes.
4. He had buzz-cut and *gimlet* eyes.
5. He had a chrome dome and *far-seeing* eyes.

EYEBROWS

bushy eyebrows	sickle shaped	crescent-of-moon shape	beetle-browed	fire worshipper-black	

154

bristly eyebrows	scythe shaped eyebrows	equinox-black eyebrows	hirsute eyebrows	Hades-black	

1. He had bushy eyebrows and a *pleasing* face.
2. He had sickle shaped eyebrows and a *shapely* face.
3. He had equinox-black eyebrows and a *seemly* face.
4. He had hirsute, bible-black eyebrows on an *artist's* face.
5. He had Hades-black eyebrows affixed to an *aesthetic* face.

NOSE

a falcon's nose	a Roman nose	a patrician nose	a raptor's nose	a lordly nose	
a hawkish nose	an imperial nose	an imperious nose	an aquiline nose	a kingly nose	

1. He had a falcon's nose and *merry* eyes.
2. He had an imperial nose and *joyful* eyes.
3. He had a patrician nose and *mirthful* eyes.
4. He had a raptor's nose and *dancing* eyes.
5. He had a lordly nose and *come-hither* eyes.

CHEEKBONES

domed cheekbones	half-dome cheekbones	arched cheekbones	pinched-in cheekbones	concave cheekbones	
defined cheekbones	half-moon cheekbones	angular cheekbones	prominent cheekbones	mountain peak cheekbones	

1. He had domed cheekbones on *tight skin*.
2. He had half-moon cheekbones on *tense skin*.
3. He had arched cheekbones on *taut skin*.
4. His pinched-in cheekbones rested on *skin that was stretched tight by exercise*.

5. His concave cheekbones rested on *skin pulled tight like a bolt of fine cloth*.

JAW

a concrete jaw	a craggy jaw	a flinty jaw	a granite jaw	an adamantine jaw	
a lantern jaw	an oaken jaw	a marble jaw	a basalt jaw	an obsidian jaw	

1. He had a lantern jaw that was *square and firm*.
2. He had a craggy jaw that was *strong and hard*.
3. He had a marble jaw that was *rugged and masculine*.
4. He had a granite jaw that was *gritty and tough*.
5. He had an obsidian jaw that was *obdurate and unyielding*.

SHOULDERS

Atlas shoulders	taurine shoulders	simian shoulders	Colossus shoulders	canyon ridge shoulders	
a Titan's shoulders	a wrestler's shoulders	Samson shoulders	Corinthian shoulders	ox yoke shoulders	

1. He had Atlas shoulders above a *six-pack*.
2. He had taurine shoulders above a *barrel chest*.
3. He had simian shoulders and an *Olympian's chest*.
4. He had Corinthian shoulders and a *horizon flat stomach*.
5. He had ox yoke shoulders and a *washboard stomach*.

STRENGTH

a gladiator's biceps	a goliath's body	a leviathan's forearms	a Spartan's muscles	a gym toned physique	
a strongman's shoulders	a Greek god's body	Popeye forearms	Schwarzenegger muscles	a gym honed physique	

1. He had a gladiator's biceps and *iron muscles*.
2. He had a goliath's body and *ironbound muscles*.
3. He had Popeye forearms and *ironclad muscles*.
4. He had a Spartan's muscles and *cast iron muscles*.
5. He had a gym honed physique and muscles *wrought from iron*.

MASCULINITY

dishy	brawny	manly	hunky	hale and hearty	
dashing	burly	strapping	handsome	hewn from rock	

1. He was dashing with *a rascal's smile*.
2. He was brawny with *a roguish smile*.
3. He was strapping with *a scamp's smile*.
4. He was hunky with *a scallywag's smile*.
5. He was hale and hearty with *a rapscallion's smile*.

MOVEMENT

a cat like grace	a tiger like tread	an athletic grace	a lion-like power	a feline grace	
a leopard like grace	sure-footed purpose	a balletic grace	a leonine poise	like a panther in slow-mo	

1. He *moved* with a cat like grace.
2. He *walked* with sure-footed purpose.
3. He *eased about* the room with a balletic grace.
4. He *prowled* around with a lion-like power.
5. He *padded* through the room like a panther in slow-mo.

USING FORMULAS

The purpose of the grid system is not to reduce the English language to a system of learning by rote exercises. Its function is fourfold.

1. To capture the **essence** of each scene, person, season or feature of nature.
2. To enable students to see the **patterns of writing** which govern English.
3. To expose them to the greatest possible amount of words that can help them **express** themselves.
4. To reintroduce a **love of nature** to a world that is increasingly technocratic.

There are most definitely faults in the book. By reducing any overlap of words to the barest possible minimum, I shackled myself in some of the chapters. Notable exceptions include the words 'sorcery' and 'sparkling', which probably occurred four or five times throughout the book. That is because they have an extraordinary ability to transform a text. It must be borne in mind, however, that I was confined to writing purely descriptive passages and essays. This brings its own problems when you are trying to avoid the monotony of starting sentences with 'It', 'The' or 'A'. I had to leave out some important factors because of the format of the book. I hope to clear those up now.

The inspiration behind the book was a question that had been burning inside me for a long time. Are people aware of the patterns of English? Do people know that lips can be described with the four 'f's'? Are they aware of the link between bells, armour, rivers and waterfalls? Do they know that fabrics can be applied to descriptions of mist, snow and darkness? I knew that the weaker the student put in front of me, the more beneficial it was for them to be able to put a structure to their work. Higher ability students also found patterns helpful when they were analysing poetry, Shakespeare and trying to compare three texts as a unit. I always showed them why and how a writer wrote what he did, not just dissecting what he wrote.

On a different note, the last century has seen three quantum technological leaps. Those were: the car, the airplane and the television/mobile phone/computer. This century shall see **nine**. The world is not an easy place for the modern student. Anything we can do as educators to help them understand and analyse the challenges ahead is a gift to them. Patterns of thought fall into this category. In a faster world, sometimes it's better to take a deep breath, slow down and try to figure out the reason behind things rather than rush headlong into the future. Then, and only then, can you say that you are thinking with stardust.

THE FORMULA FOR LIPS

FABRIC	FLOWERS	FIRE	FRUIT
satin soft	azalea soft	brazier-red	cherry sweet
silk soft	blossom soft	ember-red	cloudberry sweet
suede soft	dahlia soft	flame-red	melon sweet
velour soft	fuchsia soft	hellfire-red	peach sweet
velvet soft	petal soft	inferno-red	strawberry sweet

CLOUD, MIST, SNOW, LEAVES AND DARKNESS

cloud-adorned
cloud-blanketed
cloud-capped
cloud-clad
mist-cloaked
mist-draped
mist-festooned
mist-garlanded
mist-mantled
snow-sheathed
snow-shrouded
snow-snooded
snow-topped
darkness-veiled
darkness-wreathed

It sounds better to the ear to use some of these words in a metaphor. For example, **a veil of darkness** might be more appropriate than darkness-veiled. Whichever way a student decides, it should add to the value of a story or essay to use these terms.

Writing with Stardust

DESCRIBING MALES

BEARDS

LEVEL 1	LEVEL 2	LEVEL 3	LEVEL 4	LEVEL 5	OTHERS
a goatee	a spade shaped beard	an Abe Lincoln beard	a Captain Ahab	a Moses beard	
a galway	a devil's fork beard	a Vandyke beard	a Socratic beard	a Methuselah beard	

1. He had a **shiny** goatee.
2. He had a **smooth**, spade shaped beard.
3. He wore a **glossy**, Abe Lincoln beard.
4. He boasted a **flowing**, Socratic beard.
5. He sported a **sartorial**, Methuselah beard.

MOUSTACHES

a bushy moustache	a pencil thin moustache	a toothbrush moustache	a handlebar moustache	a Zapata moustache	
a bristly moustache	a military moustache	a smig	a walrus moustache	a D'Artegnan moustache	

1. He had a **dark**, bristly moustache.
2. He had a **dapper**, military moustache.
3. He wore a **dandy**, toothbrush moustache.
4. He wore a **drooping**, walrus moustache.
5. He sported a **dashing**, D'Artegnan moustache, the emblem of a true musketeer.

STUBBLE

dark stubble	grainy stubble	sand-rough stubble	morning shadow	a rime of grey	

| peppered stubble | gritty stubble | designer stubble | five o' clock shadow | salt and pepper stubble | |

1. He had **manly**, peppered stubble.
2. He had **manful**, gritty stubble.
3. He had **mannish**, designer stubble.
4. His face was grizzled with **manlike**, five o' clock shadow.
5. His face was grafted with a **masculine** rime of grey.

BLUE EYES

sea rover-blue eyes	nomad-blue eyes	voyager-blue eyes	seafarer-blue eyes	trailblazer-blue eyes	
Rasputin-blue eyes	nautical-blue eyes	mariner-blue eyes	wayfarer-blue eyes	wanderlust-blue eyes	

1. His Rasputin-blue eyes were **as clear as a calm lake**.
2. His nautical-blue eyes were **as clear as a summer brook**.
3. His voyager-blue eyes were **as clear as a fresh pond**.
4. His seafarer-blue eyes were **as clear as a spring stream**.
5. His trailblazer-blue eyes were **as clear as a mountain stream**.

DIFFERENT EYE COLOURS

hypnotic, meltwater-blue eyes	scorching, smaragdine-green eyes	beguiling, turquoise-green eyes	enthralling, champagne-brown eyes	enchanting, clay-grey eyes	
mesmerizing, empyrean-blue eyes	iridescent, malachite-green eyes	bewitching, tourmaline-green eyes	entrancing, molten-brown	enrapturing, loam-grey eyes	

1. He had **lambent**, meltwater-blue eyes
2. He had **fulgent**, smaragdine-green eyes.
3. He had **bedazzling**, tourmaline-green eyes.

4. He had *effulgent*, molten-brown eyes.

5. He had *scintillating*, loam-grey eyes.

SHAPE OF EYES

doe shaped eyes	saucer shaped eyes	orb round eyes	lunar shaped	moon shaped eyes	
almond shaped eyes	Saturn shaped eyes	opal round eyes	sloe shaped	millpond round	

1. They were doe shaped and *the windows to his soul*.

2. They were saucer shaped and *the mirrors of his soul*.

3. They were opal round and *the pathways to his soul*.

4. They were lunar shaped and *the gateways to his soul*.

5. They were millpond round and *the portals to his soul*.

ARCHAIC WORDS FOR EYES

a-dazzle with wonder	a-flicker with curiosity	a-gleam with delight	a-glow with love	a-sparkle with mirth	
a-fire with passion	a-flush with triumph	a-glimmer with interest	a-light with joy	a-twinkle with the 'joie de vivre'	

1. They were a-dazzle with wonder over *a friendly smile*.

2. They were a-flicker with curiosity over *a genial smile*.

3. They were a-glimmer with interest over *his affable smile*.

4. They were a-glow with love and he flashed me *an amiable smile*.

5. They were a-twinkle with the 'joie de vivre' and he graced me with *a jaunty smile*.

PERSONALITY

a dashing personality	a devil-may-care outlook	a vivacious personality	a flamboyant character	a buccaneering personality	
an	a derring-do	a gregarious	a debonair	a	

| adventurous personality | outlook | personality | character | swashbuckling personality | |

1. He had a dashing personality and *a cosmic smile*.
2. He had a devil-may-care outlook and *a stellar smile*.
3. He had a gregarious personality and *a galactic smile*.
4. He had a debonair character and *a celestial smile*.
5. He had a swashbuckling style and *an Arcadian smile*.

VOICE

| a deep voice | a bass voice | a foghorn voice | a rumbling voice | a stentorian voice | |
| a booming voice | a trombone voice | a volcanic voice | like bottled thunder | a grit-and-gravy voice | |

1. He had a booming voice, full of *vim*.
2. He had a trombone voice, full of *verve*.
3. He had a volcanic voice, loaded with *vigour*.
4. He had a voice like bottled thunder, a measure of his *vitality*.
5. He had a stentorian voice, a man who believed in '*Vi et armis*'. (*By force and arms*)

CLOTHES

| snazzy clothes | natty clothes | gap year clothes | rakish | twee clothes | |
| ritzy clothes | nifty clothes | swanky clothes | raffish clothes | Miami Vice clothes | |

1. He wore snazzy clothes and his hair was *wind-tossed*.
2. He wore natty clothes and his hair was *wind-tumbled*.
3. He wore swanky clothes and his hair was *wind-tangled*.
4. He wore raffish clothes and his hair was *wind-tousled*.
5. He wore Miami Vice clothes and his hair was *wind-tempested*.

LEVEL 1: BASIC SENTENCES

1. He had **Viking-gold** hair. **HAIR**
2. He had **bristly** eyebrows. **EYEBROWS**
3. He had a **hawkish** nose. **NOSE**
4. He had **defined** cheekbones. **CHEEKBONES**
5. He had a **concrete** jaw. **JAW**
6. He had a **Titan's** shoulders. **SHOULDERS**
7. He was **dishy**. **MASCULINITY**
8. He moved with a **leopard-like grace**. **MOVEMENT**
9. He had **sea rover-blue** eyes. **EYES**
10. They were **almond shaped**. **SHAPE OF EYES**
11. They were **a-fire with passion**. **ARCHAIC WORDS FOR EYES**
12. He was **adventurous**. **PERSONALITY**
13. He had a **deep** voice. **VOICE**
14. He wore **ritzy** clothes. **CLOTHES**
15. An **earthy scent** swirled around him. **SMELL**

LEVEL 2: A BASIC PARAGRAPH

He had a **Mohican cut** and **scythe-shaped eyebrows**. His **Roman nose** and **half-dome cheekbones** sat above an **oaken jaw**. His **wrestler's shoulders** were part of his **burly physique**. He walked with **a tiger like tread** and his **nomad-blue eyes** twinkled. They were **Saturn round** and were **a-flush with triumph** after his job promotion. His **derring-do personality** and **bass voice** were a big part of his ambitious character. He always wore **nifty clothes** and his **spicy aroma** was appealing.

LEVEL 3: CREATIVE PARAGRAPHS

He was a male model and he was adored by the fairer sex for his **Teutonic-gold hair**. It was a casual jumble sometimes but mostly neat and flowing. His **crescent-of-moon eyebrows** were thin and narrow. He carried an **imperious nose** well and his **angular cheekbones** carved down towards a **flinty jaw**. Unusually for a model, he had a **manly**, **Samson physique**. The catwalk loved the way he glided with **an athletic grace** without skipping a beat.

His **mariner-blue eyes** were **orb round** and darted constantly, **a-gleam with delight** and the vigour of youth. They were soft, Irish eyes and swam with joy. They shone brightly, like two sapphires dipped in milky pools. Everyone commented on his **vivacious** character and his gentle nature. His voice could be **foghorn loud** when he was booming out a guffaw but it was normally mellifluous. His **gap year clothes** always made him appear younger than his years. The swirl of his loamy cologne had them swooning in the aisles.

LEVEL 4: ADVANCED PARAGRAPHS

He wasn't a male model but he should have been. The lush, **mother lode-gold hair** he groomed so carefully had a rippling quality, a sign of his rude health. His only blemish was that he was **beetle-browed** and they sometimes knitted in frustration. The **aquiline nose** he sported complemented his **prominent cheekbones**. **Handsome** in an understated way, his **basalt jaw** and **Spartan shoulders** spoke of strength. He possessed a latent, **leonine power** and always walked with purpose and authority.

People had always remarked that his best feature was his entrancing, **wayfarer-blue eyes**. **Sloe shaped**, they could shine as bright as the evening stars when they were **a-light with joy**. At other times, they could resemble two liquid-blue pools of flashing fire. **Flamboyant of character**, the room always filled with his sonorous, **rumbling voice**. He was also quick to crack a joke or fire off a humorous retort. His **rakish clothes** were a source of amusement to some, not least because they emanated an herbal smell.

LEVEL 5: COMPLEX WRITING: DIFFERENT PEOPLE

A Brad Pitt look-alike: The man I met at the wedding had a touch of the Brad Pitt about him. His hair was **Achilles-gold** and coiffed to perfection. His eyes had the same startling clarity as a mountain stream and the lineaments of his face were in perfect proportion to each other. He seemed moulded from a different cast as he had an androgynous look uncommon to most people. Lacquered and enamelled by the sun, he radiated energy and brio. His **mountain peak cheekbones** appeared chiselled into shape by a master craftsman. They were of such sharp contours, it looked as if they were sculpted and pared to perfection. With eyes as bright and **spellbinding** as lode stars, they bewitched all those who fell under his steady gaze. They were **a-sparkle with mirth** and **shone like two eternity-blue jewels** enwrought in snow.

He had a fruity laugh and a **grit-and-gravy voice**. It alternated from strident to soothing depending on his whim. The trace of a southern drawl was in there also but the brogue itself was a gentle one and pleasing to the ear. He moved with **a feline grace**. It looked as if he was padding across the ground rather than walking. His **oval face** held a pleasant countenance and spoke of a gentle soul. When he flashed those sorcery-white, piano key teeth, he could melt hearts. Unusually, his eyebrows were **arched and seam-gold**, not the bristly, fire gazer black common to most men. He carried himself with a kingly air, a distinct mood of gravitas, although he could be **buccaneering and childlike** on occasion. His twee clothes bore this out. His eau-de-Cologne left a vapour trail of spice and cinnamon behind him when he walked.

DESCRIBING THE RAIN

SPRING	SUMMER	AUTUMN	WINTER
airy rain	beads of rain	**hissing** rain	Amazonian showers
drizzling rain	dewdrops of rain	**saturating** rain	a biblical **deluge**
evanescent rain	droplets of rain	**seething** rain	monsoon rains
mist-like rain	pearls of rain	**shredding** rain	Noah's-Ark-lavish
mizzling rain	*****ploppy** drops of	**sibilant** rain	**sluicing** rains
pitter-patter of rain	plump drops of	**sissing** rain	**torrential** rainfall
showering rain	pregnant drops of	**sizzling** rain	silver icicles of rain
spraying rain	**splattering** rain	**soaking** rain	silver nails of rain
sprinkling sound of rain	the **susurration** of rain	**spitting** rain	upside-down rain (so heavy it bounces upwards)
tinkling rain	teardrops of rain	stinging rain	the billion-fold **ping**

The words that are highlighted in bold are onomatopoeic words. The word *'ploppy' is technically not a word, but it sounds so right for raindrops I just had to put it in!

Now that you have your word banks for the seasonal nature of rain, it is time to concentrate more on its sound. All the onomatopoeic words you need to describe rain falling are on the next page.

SOFT RAIN SOUNDS	**HEAVY RAIN SOUNDS**
The rain was:	The rain was:

burbling (gurgling) into the drains.	**boiling** the surface of the river.
dripping from the flowers.	**buzzing** incessantly with noise.
chinking off the windows.	**dinging** furiously off the tin roof.
clinking off the cars.	**drumming** off the tarmacadam.
making a lovely, **lilting** sound.	**fizzing** against the top of the bus.
murmuring like white noise.	**hammering** off their leather jackets.
plinking off the puddles.	**ker-plunking** off the swollen pools.
strumming against the roof tops.	**pinging** angrily against the glass.
suspiring (sighing) through the air.	**plunking** onto the muddy earth.
swishing off my skin.	**smashing** onto the heads of the crowd.
thrumming off the cobble stones.	*****swooshing** onto the flooded fields.
weaving (moving side to side) with the wind.	**tapping** madly off the door.
whirring (a rapid buzz) off the leaves.	**thunking** the tops of the trees.
gently **whisking** (stirring) the lake's surface.	**whizzing** from the sky.
whispering in the air.	**whooshing** as the heavens opened.

'Swooshing' is not a word either, although it should be! The next step is to think up of a scene or situation where you can use the words and sentences above. A simple example might look like the paragraphs on the next page.

LEVEL 1

I looked out the window. The sky was tar-black and the large clouds were moving towards me. I heard a tapping on the window and then it became a pitter-patter. People ran for cover outside and umbrellas were opened as the clouds spat out their beads of water. Puddles began plinking as the rainfall became heavier. The roofs of the cars danced with spray and I could hear the murmuring of the rain through the window. It sounded like the buzzing of angry bees.

For a Level 2 assignment, more detail should be added. Imagine the effect of the rain on the trees and include more detail on the sky and clouds. At the end of the paragraph, try to write something about the sun coming out. This will vary your writing style.

LEVEL 2

I quickened my pace as the clouds began to gather in the sky. Up to now, the sky had been postcard-perfect, but it was changing. The beautiful cocktail-blue shade was beginning to darken into gravel-grey. Large pillows of cloud were forming, blotting out the old-gold colour of the sun.

I got the first splatter of rain when I was halfway across the meadow. I took shelter under an old oak, hoping that I could see out the shower. Droplets of moisture began to drip from the leaves. They were sprinkling onto the grass like a gardener's hose. Then the rainfall became more intense. A wall of rain moved over the oak and the drops were drumming against the canopy. So much rain was falling that the sound blurred into one long, whirring noise. It reminded me of the rotor blades on a helicopter. Eventually, the noise lessened and the drops faded into a musical chime.

The sun came out again, casting slanted beams of light across the meadow. Steam rose slowly from the grass. It rose up eerily and drifted mist-like towards the molten-gold sun. The image was so vivid that it stayed with me all the way home.

Level 3 should conjure up a scene where the rain's effect can be explored in more detail. The words should get more complex also. An idea might be to visualise a forest scene in autumn, for example. Transport yourself there and describe the colours, the sensations and the sounds of the rain.

LEVEL 3

It began as a whispering in the air. The day had been beautiful and the sky was like a dome of plasma-blue. The clouds had looked like airy anvils drifting under the gleaming disc of sun. We had put our tent up just before the Reaper's moon of autumn appeared over the trees. The moon seemed to turn the leaves into a flaming patchwork of colours: scorching-yellows, lava-reds and burnished-browns. It added an alien glamour to a perfect scene. We heard a greedy thrush, snail a-tapping on rock; he finished his supper before fluttering into the owl-light of the forest. The mournful cry of a lonely fox echoed through the vault-still silence of the trees. A huffing wind rose up then, stirring the flaps of our tent. A tinkling sound came to our ears as the first pearls of rain dropped onto the leaves. The sound was like the glassy clinking of a champagne flute, lilting and clear. A sheet of rain passed over us and the sound intensified. The noise on the tent was like the phut-phut-phut that ripened nuts make when they hit the ground. It wasn't the soft, sodden, swollen drops of spring we were hearing; it was like ball-bearings were hitting the canvas roof with force. We could also hear an occasional ker-plunking sound. It was caused by the rainwater gathered on the tent falling to the ground in a great swash of release.

The thermometer plunged as we huddled together and shivered in the tent. For a brief moment, we thought that we might be doomed adventurers, destined to get swept away in a mighty flood. We needn't have worried. The curtain of rain passed over by the time dawn arrived. An explosion of birdsong erupted from the dripping trees and it was if the rain had never been.

A Level 4 assignment might involve a degree of philosophy. You can discuss how the rain is both life giving and life threatening. The metaphors should be more creative and the turn of phrase made more enriching.

LEVEL 4

'The sun enables life. The rain grants it safe passage'.

The winter sky is a widow's sky, bedarkened and weeping. The clouds are churlish and kraken-cruel. They cough out great gouts of water and thunking balloons of sopping moisture. It teems down in a biblical deluge, flooding the rivers, drowning the fields and overflowing the dams. It is a Noah's-Ark cataclysm of rain, an unending cataract of water sluicing from the sky. Trees are uprooted, cars go bobbing by and entire villages disappear under a frothy lather of suds. Cities are overwhelmed and electricity blackouts have people living in fear of the unknown. The rain is incessant. It snaps and crackles like bracken pods in a bush fire. The flood-gates in the sky have been opened and no-one is there to close them back up, it seems.

Is this the scene from a sci-fi movie? Is it a terrifying vision of a future world? Indeed it is not. It is the new reality for people from Missouri to Manchester, from Mumbai to Melbourne. The rain is man's new enemy, according to news reports. It is public enemy number one. It has betrayed man and is now the most destructive arrow in nature's quiver. The rain has a bad 'rep' at the moment. Is this how it should be viewed? Maybe we are forgetting the gifts it bestows upon us.

The spring sky is a fragile, pellucid-blue. The clouds are frail and angel-white. They are carried on a light, ruffling breeze. The soil of Mother Earth is titanium hard and in need of nourishment. A misty rain falls down. It is as frail as a Scottish smirr and its misty dew feels like warm butter melting on a face. As it falls, it unlocks the glassy fingers of winter's frosty fist, one by one. Flowers slowly unfurl in the meadows and ripple like coral arms at low tide. The rivers exhale with a murmurous purr of satisfaction. The spring rains are here and they are as sinless and glistening as an angel's tears.

The summer sky is neon-blue and vibrant. The sun-crisped flowers of the meadow are wilting. They gape at the tufty clouds and beg for their parched petals to be given one more shot of insulin. The clouds oblige and rain descends in little gleam-drops of silver. If you were to stand in the meadow, the drops would feel as sparkly and effervescent as champagne bubbles hitting your skin. The sound of the rain is a harmonic thrumming, nature's white noise. Silver trickles of water seep into the soil, renewing the life-roots of the plants beneath. A homely, baked-earth smell rises from the land as it is washed and cleansed by the dewy tears of summer rain. Petrichor, the smell of the first rains after a dry spell, rises like a miasma. It is a jasmine-and-gingerbread fragrance, warm and fresh, and it laves the land with sweetness. The farmer is happy. The rain has giveth what the sun would taketh away.

The autumn sky is dark and vengeful. Steaming shrouds of cloud coil and writhe. Then an unearthly caterwauling sound fills the air. The wind whips up into frenzy. It is a shrieking, keening omen of the carnage to follow. The clouds race across the sky, thrumming with the charged energy they are desperate to release. It starts with big, sopping drops of moisture. They are wild and indiscriminate, plump missiles of mass destruction that splatter onto the soft soil. The topsoil turns into slushy goo, but it doesn't matter. The harvest has been taken in and the farmer stokes the glowing coals with a poker and a sigh of contentment. The rain is sissing and hissing off the roof, teeming onto the spongy earth. The farmer thinks about how most gifts come with a cost. He shudders at the thought of another winter, but counts his blessings that the rain has once again ensured his livelihood.

To him, the rain is the nectar of the gods and the serum of the sky. He is neither philosopher nor ancient mariner, neither writer nor jungle adventurer, yet he understands the importance of nature's bounty.

If beauty is God's signature, then rain is his final flourish.

A Level 5 passage may include the rain only as an incidental event in the story. It could have a central hero or anti-hero (a man/woman with bad characteristics doing some good or vice versa). The plot should contain a theme or moral and the use of metaphor/simile/pathetic fallacy should be advanced. Above all, it should be enjoyable to read.

Level 5: The Crime o' the Ancient Mariner

"**The water, like a witch's oils,**
 Burnt green, and blue, and white."
The Rime of the Ancient Mariner: Samuel Coleridge.

An ancient mariner was, in times of yore, a sea-gazer. That, at least, is the common perception.

Many people today, however, see the mariner from a snuff-induced perspective. They envision him as a doughty lad, his hand clasped to the tiller, his far-seeing eyes scanning the horizon for signs which mere mortals could not fathom. His hair is windswept and hobbit-curled, his skin is a healthy, kelp-brown and he has eyes of the deepest, Atlantis-blue. He carries himself with an easy grace and he is ruminating on fate and empires. Tacking gently into the nuzzling breeze, his nostrils inhale the mesh of pelagic scents. Moon glades appear on the sea every so often. When the rickety clouds disappear, their bright, pearly pools of glow make his soul rejoice. The sea itself is a winding-sheet of silver and the opaline light of the moon makes it shimmer with a tightened beauty. Stars fizz and shoot across the night sky like the faerie-fire mentioned in dusty tomes. Oh to be an ancient mariner.

The truth, unfortunately, is somewhat different. The mariner, you see, was not quite the romantic we think of him today. He was not so much a seafarer as a sea-fearer.

His hand is gripping the tiller with abject terror. His sea roving eyes spy a whirlpool developing and churning beneath his feet. He fears it is the doom-crack of the world and that he will fall over and into it. His little boat bucks and bobs. It is a strain to keep it from being cloven asunder by the white fangs of the vortex and the sanded teeth of the reefs. His feet slip and slide on the deck made slick by fish guts and spilled rum. The moon is carbuncle-red, the blood moon of October, and it leers down at him over the shocking clap of the waves. The stars do not register because he wears the stunned, slack-jawed expression of a mooncalf. His eyes slowly widen and gaze down into the boundless depths of his doom. His eyes are sprat-wide with terror.

This ancient mariner is a bootlegger and the sea is his enemy. For many years now, he has taken to describing the sea in terms normally applied to the accursed.

To him, the sea is a heaving salt coffin made by the ark wright of the Gods. The spray washes over him like a sea-spectre's breath. The rain is as hot as a hellcat's spit, bitter and stinging. The air itself is a burning brine-shroud, making his eyes bleed with salt. Thunder booms out like a dragon's cough, high and rumbling. The lightning is as splayed as mandrake roots and the foam-flecked waves are like a madman's slobber. The mist is the devil's milk, clotting his mind and clawing at the air. To him, shooting stars are the sizzling sparks from sprite-fire. He has to take care not to be hit by one. The fog is Lucifer's grog, chafing and cutting his skin. He is mindful not to inhale too much of it. The clouds are necromancer-black and wear the garb of the damned. He is wary of becoming like them, drifting into infinity, nameless and valueless.

And yet, there was a time when this bootlegger was a future mariner. When he was a little boy, his father used to take him seafaring in his one-mast cutter. There he would huddle amongst the cargo, gazing up at the stars, with the hull creaking raw, the rigging rippling and the rum casks heaving. Under the light of a moon bow, the ocean became as still and flat as a tarn and it burned blue and green and white, burning with the brightness of an alchemist's oils. The barnacles on the boat used to shine like bucklers and the smell of tar and rope, of teak and rum was like snuff for the soul. The elemental hymn of sea and boat was pleasant, a harmonic rhapsody of swell, jingle and creak. Then, when the wind was low, the waves hushed and the water lulled, he would learn the ways of the sea from his father.

Everything was expressed in minimalist English, with neither ornament nor gloss. Everything was made simple. Thus, the waves we now call rollers, whitecaps, breakers and combers were given simple names. He learned of scroll-waves and barrel-waves, curlicues and tubes. There were wave-billows and bellows, wave-furrows and hollows, all of them designed to send you to a watery perdition of no return. He learned of the sky, how there were woolpacks and thunderheads, wolf moons and cloudbursts. He learned how the fool-strewn sea floor had been scooped out by Neptune's leviathan hand and that now it stretched down into infinity. He learned of the haunting emptiness of the sea and how it could never leave the soul once it had navigated its way in. Finally, everything was caulked down into one oath, one vow; never to sail under a blood moon. For the blood moon is no honey moon; the sea under it is a cruel bride.

Then his father had died. It was from a locker of reasons, not just one, but chiefly the lung rot. The chink of coin had died with him, the windfall ripeness of life turned to fester, and the family slowly starved. He and his brothers fell on hard times and turned to brigandage, plundering up and down the King's highway. Two of them had been caught and were forced to dance the Tyburn jig down London way, the day before Cromwell was disinterred and danced his. The image of them dangling and swaying from the gallows had driven him back to the bosom of the sea, where a man could make a dishonest living in peace. Now he was here, dancing under a blood moon himself, with a mistress and unborn child awaiting him at the shingled cove and the hole from hell at his feet.

Many years later, a black-clad lady would go into the village inn of a blood moon. Men with woollen hats and cruel laughs would mutter into their glasses and curse her name when she entered. She would sit in the corner 'till the clock chimed 10 to midnight, defying them with her presence. Then, when the tallow burned dull and the frothy mugs low; when darkness shut mouths and the fire dim glowed; a lone voice rose from among the shadows. She would sing a mournful sea shanty in a plaintive voice, pregnant with anguish and longing. She always started it with an exclamation: "o!" and their hackles rose as their souls froze. A few of the men would get up and leave.

"The wind howled long, the sea growled wrong,

The night that my Jack cried.

No aid came from within the inn

The night that my Jack died."

"That's enough of that, now, Mary," said the innkeeper. "He's not coming back and neither should you."

"A pox on all of ye," she hissed and left the same way she came in.

Jack knew it would be a rough passage home. The sea was too placid for a sanguine moon. There was a storm a-brewing.

The boat began to roll from side to side and the temperature dipped all of a sudden. Dark clouds obscured the moon. They churned grimly in the night sky, as black as a witch's Sabbath. The moon's mercury flush was painted silver by the thunderheads, casting down shivers of light with a ghostly glow. Underneath the moon, the rain moved towards him like a wraith's veil of sorrow. A winnowing wind fermented and sighed, rippling the surface of the corpse calm sea. Thunder clapped. It boomed out, leaving a concussed silence after it. The sea itself was tomb silent. Then the rising wind rasped his sails and made them flap jaggedly. Kinked lightning wriggled from the sky and fizzled with a golden sheen. A yowling sound rolled across the arch of heaven, tumbling out like the rocky echo of a cavern. His boat heaved and tossed in the rising swell and he gripped the tiller with his naked fingers. He could just make out the figure of his wife standing on the shingled beach, lamp raised aloft to guide him home. Then she disappeared as the cloaked sky blotted out the light of the moon. The rain-shroud passed by, spitting at him with its Undead tears. It wrung his hobbit curls into a mop and soaked his jerkin through. He could smell his own fear as the fumes rose from his clothes, a mixture of sea mongrel and must. A monster's cough bellowed in the sky and it sounded like all the hunting hounds of hell were unleashed together to kill him. War trumpets followed in their wake, blaring out like the clarion call of the condemned. The rain whipped down like crystal nails and streaky lightning emblazoned the sky. The sea swells rose and his beard rime froze as the north wind blew and sped him to his doom. Lacerating rain stung his bare arms like ice burn and the sea throbbed grey with woe. His boat bobbed like a cork upon the capacious sea and for the first time ever, he felt his own mortality. The brine hissed and sissed, lashing his face, and he felt a fever in his eyes. His little boat keeled and tilted like the death flop of a mackerel. The timber planks buckled and bulged, then screaked and shuddered, but the boat righted herself once more.

The bedlam of the sea caused a hectic in his blood, but he could swear that an old man's, spectral face was fixed in the sky where the moon should be. It wore a mask of hatred and longing and it transfixed Jack utterly. He looked at it aghast, like a mooncalf would stare at the night sky. The old man's eyes seemed to glare at the sea on his starboard side. Jack's own eyes followed and slowly widened as he gazed down into a whirlpool opening and spinning beneath the boat. The words of his father came to him unbidden then: "There's nothing worse than the dreadful curse lodged in a dead man's eye."

Jack became angry, trying to remember the rest of the advice. He knew it was important, but he couldn't think with the tumult and the tempest. A few lines of poesy his father had taught him sprang up instead. He clenched the tiller tighter with his numb left hand, straining with all his might to defy the whirlpool, and shook his fist at the old man with the other, crying out above the wind:

Ochon, ochon, o! o! ochon,

Ochon on a wide, wide sea;

But that's a song she'll never sing,

'till I'm in perfidy."

The whirlpool spun faster and wider, sucking Jack into the doom-crack of the world. The old man's eyes burned brighter, hypnotising Jack with their intensity. He shook his head, as if casting off a glamour. Jack let go of the tiller, raising both his fists in defiance of his fate and screamed up at the apparition:

"I know thee, Ancient Mariner,

I know thy skinny hand,

(And know thee too, thy grey-beard loon)

Come oath or curse or vow or Hell,

I'll make the shingled sand."

The sea boiled and churned like a cannibal's cauldron. It heaved and bulged, pushing up giant waves from the fathomless gullet of its depths. The wind screamed like a banshee's wail and whipped at his face. Jack's two hands gripped the tiller and refused to let go. His father's words came back unbidden; "A true mariner never deserts a sinking ship." He gripped on tighter. A mountainous wave rose up before him, blotting out the sky. The wind howled out his doom, the whirlpool span faster and whiter and the old man's face leered down in triumph. The boat rose with the swell, inclining upwards to its destruction. It was propelled up onto the lip and hovered there, a fly-speck on the cobwebbed lines of the wave. Time seemed suspended. The whirlpool gaped under him with dire-white jaws. It roiled and spun, inviting Jack in. Then the boat plummeted down into its milky depths, swallowed whole in a final, terrible, squeak of timber.

The waves subsided and the sea stilled. A terrible silence followed, and then a head rose from the surf. Jack swam towards his wife with steady stokes, following the light all the way to the shingled cove.

"I ran to the inn for help but no-one would come," she said.

"That's all right, Mary," he said. "I never liked the Mariners Inn anyway."

"How did you survive *that*?" she asked, looking at the timbers washing up on the slurpy shore.

"Promise me one thing first, Mary. Don't go back to the inn again."

"We'll see," she said doubtfully. "Answer my question."

"There's only one thing worse than the dreadful curse lodged in a dead man's eye," he said.

"And that's taking bad advice." He paused and then for effect, he added. "Mariners be damned. I jumped."

DESCRIBING THE SUN

When describing the sun, there are 5 simple ways to do it. These are: the shape using *a metaphor*, *the reflection*, *the colour*, *weapons* and *water*. Then you are using an 'artist's eye' in order to portray the sun and its beams in a different way. We will start with 10 metaphors for the shape.

10 *metaphors* for the shape:

1. … a fiery ball in the sky.

2. … a glowing medallion in the sky.

3. … a golden globe in the sky.

4. … God's morning star (i.e. the sunrise).

5. … the celestial fireball in the sky.

6. … a heavenly orb.

7. … Titan's fiery wheel.

8. … the God-goldened disc in the sky.

9. … God's golden eye.

10. … God's luminous daystar.

These are just some examples of possible metaphors to be used. The next step is to apply the *reflection* of the sun to the metaphors. The best 5 are probably:

blazing	flaming	glowing	shining	scorching

You can also use **archaic words** which will lend a sense of age and antiquity to the sentence. 5 examples of this are:

a-gleam	a-dazzle	a-glint	a-glitter	a-shine

Now 10 *colours* relating to yellow or gold may be used. Some interesting ones are:

honeycomb-yellow	saffron-yellow	waxmelt-yellow	molten-gold	gloriole-gold
ore gold-yellow	yolk-yellow	ingot-gold	motherlode-gold	auriole-gold

The final step is to link all of these into a sentence using terms to do with **weapons** and **water**. For example, underneath are 5 terms of each for you to use.

1. *Arrows* of sunlight *bathed* the meadow.

2. *Hafts* of sunlight *drowned* the valley.

3. *Lances* of sunlight *splashed* the forest's floor.

4. *Shafts* of light *poured* onto the lake.

5. *Spears* of light *showered* the lonely moor.

All the techniques can then be joined into a short paragraph in order to make your writing more effective. Underneath is the finished product:

I walked through the forest. The sun above me was blazing like Titan's fiery wheel in the sky. It was a-dazzle with splendour and it was a soul-swelling experience. Between gaps in the forest's canopy, lances of its molten-gold beams splashed onto the floor. In places, the dead leaves seemed to be a-fire with an inner glow.

That is just one example of how to give your writing a more interesting slant. Using a different grouping of words, you can write the following:

I sat down by a glass-clear lake. The sun was like a celestial fireball in the sky. Its beams were scorching the land and sent the lake a-glitter with golden sparkles. In the afternoon, it began to get cloudy. The sun was a muted, waxmelt-yellow but shafts of light still poured through patches of cloud and onto the lake. Speckled trout arced into the air and plopped onto the water's surface, seeking to grab a fly from the platoons of them hanging over the lake.

DESCRIBING THE MOON

	American Indian	Medieval English	Colonial American	Others
January	wolf	wolf	winter's	Ice moon **(neo pagan)**
February	snow	storm	trapper's	Budding moon **(Chinese)**
March	worm	chaste	fish	Death moon **(neo pagan)**
April	pink	seed	planter's	moon of Awakening **(Celtic)**
May	flower	hair	milk	Dragon moon **(Chinese)**
June	strawberry	dyad	rose	moon of Horses **(Celtic)**
July	blood	mead	summer	Hungry Ghost **(Chinese)**
August	sturgeon	wort	dog day's	Lightning moon **(neo pagan)**
September	corn	barley	harvest	Singing moon **(Celtic)**
October	hunter's	blood	hunter's	Blood moon **(neo pagan)**
November	beaver	fog	beaver	Dark moon **(Celtic)**
December	cold	oak	Christmas	Long Night **(neo pagan)**

The wolves howl mournfully outside the village, slinking between shadows and the dark shape of the tents. A bitter, winter-white moon hangs in the sky and the smoke from dying fires still lingers in the air. A pile of buffalo bones lie to one side, gleaming silver and attracting the ravenous wolves. It is January 16, 1621. In exactly two months to the day, an Indian named Samoset will walk into an encampment at Maine, New England with the words: "Welcome, Englishmen!" They give him a coat and he will trade furs and fish with the pilgrims of the Mayflower. Life for the Indians will never be the same again.

The similarity between the moon-names of the pilgrims from Plymouth fleeing persecution and the native Indians is fascinating. One can trace the development of their traditions, culture and hunting/farming habits from the terms applied. Underneath are some explanations of the most difficult:

1. **Worm moon**: so called because the worms used to leave trails in the melting snow.

2. **Dyad moon**: from the word duo, meaning two, when the sun and moon appeared in the sky together.

3. **Mead moon**: named after a drink of honey and ale used for celebrations. Hunting for honey sounds dangerous!

4. **Harvest moon**: named after the medieval word 'haerfest', meaning autumn. A celebration usually occurred around September 23rd after the last 'mell' or sheaf of corn was brought in. Hence the term 'pell-mell', meaning crazy! Playing 'hooky', meaning absent, comes from this era also.

5. **Wort moon**: named after healing plants such as butterwort and woundwort which grew at this time.

6. **Sturgeon moon**: Indians around the Great Lakes were able to catch the huge fish, the sturgeon, which were active at this time.

7. **Dog day's moon**: The Roman's named it thus originally after Sirius, the Dog Star. It was traditionally the hottest time of the year and dogs either went mad or collapsed with exhaustion.

8. **Blood moon**: so named because the moon can appear red at certain times.

9. **Blue moon**: It became popular as a term after an article was published in the 'Sky and Telescope' in March 1946. I'm inclined to believe the theory that it comes from the word 'belewe', however, an old Saxon word meaning 'beware' (as in beware the false moon). A blue moon does occur once every 2-3 years. This is because the **lunar month** is 11 days shorter than the calendar month (**29.53 days** in a month). Hence, every two and a half years or so, there is an 'extra' moon. There are 13 moons instead of 12. Monks used to have to convince the populace on the occurrence of a 'bewere' moon that they had to fast for another month for Lent! Monks also caused the extinction of the beaver moon term. Beaver and turtle were classed as aquatic animals in England so that the monks could eat them on Fridays. Blue moons **can** exist to the naked eye. In 1950 and 1951, forest fires in Sweden and Canada scattered the red and yellow light particles, turning the moon blue for those watching it. The same happened after the Krakatoa volcano in 1883.

10. **Dark moon**: There is no such thing as the dark side of the moon. Dark spots on the moon can be seen from earth, however. These are caused by old lava beds and meteor impacts, which are grey on the moon but appear as dark spots to us.

For the purposes of descriptive writing, being able to put in a term like a wolf moon adds a touch of exotica and spice to a passage. I love the Reaper's moon, personally, when the corn or wheat was brought in by the reapers. The section on OTHERS in the grid has capital letters because the choice is up to the writer to decide if they should be capitalised or not.

The moon is perhaps the 'magic pill' of imagery when you want to create an evocative scene. Everyone has their own idea on what makes for a great moon image. It could be a shimmering, globe-gold moon. It could be the eerie, blood-red harvest moon of autumn or the dreaded death moon of March. This post will show how to use a silver moon in an atmospheric way. In particular, it will show how to use a silver sea-moon. If you want evoke a beautiful image and make your writing compelling, this is the moon for you! There are no rules to descriptive writing. However, there are some useful hints that you might take on board. For example, it is easier to divide the moon into the following categories: *shape, colour, reflection, metaphors for the moonbeams* and *similes.*

Suggested *shapes* are the following:

an orb	a disc	a halo	a ring	a salver

The *colours* are completely up to you but some nice silvers are to be found with metals.

alloy-silver	argent-silver	nickel-silver	orris-silver	zinc-silver

You could be more creative and try using ghostly silvers for an eerie scene or others even more creative. Here are some examples:

1. ghostly-silver or dewgleam-silver

2. phantom-silver or diamond-flame silver

3. spectre-silver or hoarfrost-silver

4. spooky-silver or solar-silver

5. wraith-silver or sequin-silver

The best 5 *reflective* verbs for the moon are:

gleaming	glinting	glowing	shimmering	glimmering

Then it is just a simple case of using creative **metaphors for the moonbeams**. Here are 5 of the best:

1. chords of moonlight

2. harpstrings of moonlight

3. ribbons of moonlight

4. strands of moonlight

5. tendrils of moonlight

The final stage of the process is to use *similes* that contain these words or similar words. It is important to note that, as always, this process is only a **guide to developing an 'artist's eye'**. I don't claim to know it all by any means. However, the hints given should inspire the readers to think about their own creativity and attempt to better the sentences below. Underneath are some nice expressions for a sea-moon using the formula.

1. The moon was like a ghostly-silver orb in the sky. Its beams spilled across the sea *like lines of glittering fire*. It was an alluring scene.

2. The moon was like a phantom-silver disc in the sky. Chords of moonlight lasered across the sea *like lines of glimmering fire*. It was a captivating scene.

3. The moon was like a spectre-silver halo in the sky. Ribbons of light rebounded off the mirrored surface of the sea *like silver tracers of fire*. It was soul-enriching.

4. The moon was like a spook-silver ring in the sky. Its ghostly light shimmered on the water, silvering the sea *like rippling aluminium*. It was an entrancing sight.

5. **The moon was like a wraith-silver salver hanging in the lonely sky. Tendrils of moonlight, as bright as diamond-flame, turned the sea a-glow** like melted platinum. **It was as if I was watching a scene from an old fable stepping off the page and I was beguiled by its beauty. The Chinese called the May moon the dragon moon and I could see why. The waves were a-glitter like curved scales and I became lost in the haunting lullaby of their swell and sigh.**

DESCRIBING THE STARS

For the stars, you should again focus on four main aspects: the **colour**, the **reflection**, the **shape** and using an effective **simile**. This comes back to the concept of looking at the world with an 'artist's eye'.

A child loves the way the stars are twinkling like little pulses of light. They also love drawing stars as there is symmetry to the five sides that other shapes don't have. As well as this, it is the first shape they will draw which gives them a sense of achievement because of its complexity. If you think of it, a square, circle or triangle is relatively easy. Drawing a star, however, exercises parts of the brain that haven't been used before. Starting at the bottom left, they have to go up, down, up and across, across, then down and across. I often wonder how many teachers actually show them how to do this. I'm pretty certain that it would save a child a lot of time were they to be shown how to trace a star properly from first day. If not, then a lot of stars would have to be drawn in ignorance before achieving success.

These posts I'm uploading hope to achieve the same. Make your students **think of the different components** that make up descriptive writing. Whether it be the branch of a tree that is compared to a similar shape or the texture of flowers, nearly everything in nature has a colour, shape, action (or inaction, like a womb-still lake) and sensation/smell associated with it. Every English student should be able to grasp that essential fact. It then makes it so much easier to evoke a sensory piece of descriptive writing for the reader. If they are not taught that, they may end up like the child trying to draw a star while other children in the class are moving on to complex octagons.

5 different colours for the stars:

birthstone-blue	molten-gold	solar-yellow	sequin-silver	polar-white

The reflection of the stars:

flashing and flickering	gleaming and glittering	sparkling and shimmering	twinkling and dazzling	glistering and pulsing

The stars are similar in shape to:

| snowflakes | pinpricks | asters | petals | pentagrams |

5 creative similes for the stars. The stars looked:

1. ...like scattered moondust in the sky.

2. ...like a large hand had tossed diamond dust into the sky.

3. ...like beacons of hope for all the lost souls of the world.

4. ... like bejewelled grains of sand allowed to sparkle in silence.

5. ...like the glittering sparks from angelfire.

The final step is to pick out which words and phrases you like the best and put them together into a sentence. Also try to pick a remote location for your setting where the stars would be most vividly seen. We will give you an example using the ocean. You are lost at sea. Are the stars comforting and a sign of hope or are they making you pine for civilisation? Are they the streetlamps of nature or are they a flashing reminder of your own fleeting mortality? The story is up to you, but by using our formulas you should come up with something like this:

The waves glopped and slashed off the wooden raft. Then the full moon came out and the wave-motion died down. It was an eerie, spectre-silver moon. Its ghostly lustre sent beams of argent-silver spilling across the sea. The wraith-like light flooded the sea, making it glow like silvered mercury.

Stars winked at me from the endless arch of void-black beyond the moon's corona. In places they were birthstone-blue and beautiful, all a-glitter in their heavenly finery. The ones furthest away, almost outside the span of human comprehension, were like flashing pinpricks in a veil of darkness. They had a faint, silver tint and they looked like they were the distant, glittering sparks from angel fire. All of them were beacons of hope for all the lost souls of the world, or so I thought. It seemed to me that there was a snowfall sparkling in outer space and I felt privileged to witness it.

A QUICK REFERENCE GUIDE

SPRING

FIELD COLOURS	SOFT SOUNDS	FLOWERY SMELLS	SPIRITUAL SENSATIONS	HEAVENLY TASTES
Amazon-green	the baa-baa of lambs	aloe Vera sweet	soul embracing	ambrosial
aphid-green	the babbling of brooks	balsamic sweet	soul bolstering	angelic
carnival-green	the bumbling of bees	blossom sweet	soul cherishing	Arcadian
chartreuse-green	the burbling of streams	calamine sweet	soul comforting	celestial
garland-green	the buzzing of midges	honeysuckle sweet	soul cultivating	cherubic
jasper-green	the carolling of the dawn chorus	jasmine sweet	soul lulling	divine
pea-green	the cheeping of chicks	meadow sweet	soul nourishing	empyreal
parsley-green	the chiming of cataracts	myrrh sweet	soul nurturing	godlike
sap-green	the chirring of grasshoppers	pollen sweet	soul refreshing	seraphic
watercress-green	the drizzling of raindrops	rosewater sweet	soul stoking	supernal

SPRING

MEADOW COLOURS	SOFT SOUNDS	SUGARY SMELLS	SPIRITUAL SENSATIONS	TASTE ADJECTIVES
brochure-green	the exhaling of the wind	baked apple	spirit boosting	appetizing
fable-green	the humming of lawnmowers	candied	spirit enhancing	delectable
fantasy-green	the intoning of bumble bees	confectionary	spirit enkindling	delicious
fairyland-green	the mizzling of the rain	dewy	spirit ennobling	exquisite
fairytale-green fantasia-green	the plinking of waterfalls	honeyed	spirit enriching	extravagant
Jurassic-green	the puffing of the wind	nectarine	spirit lifting	intoxicating
postcard-green	the orinasal hum of bees	saccharine	spirit raising	lavish
storybook-green	the rustling of grass	syrupy	spirit refreshing	luscious
wonderland-green	the shush over the land	tutti-fruity	spirit renewing	lush

SPRING

HEAVENLY VALLEYS	SOFT SOUNDS	SWEET SMELLS	PHYSICAL SENSATIONS	TASTE ADJECTIVES
Arcadian-green	the sighing of zephyrs	blancmange sweet	eye-opening	luxuriant
Babylon-green	the snipping of shears	caramel sweet	eye-widening	mouth watering
Eden-green	the sobbing of streams	gelatin sweet	goose bump-inducing	opulent
Elysium-green	the sploshing of trout	glucose sweet	hair-raising	ravishing
Jerusalem-green	the swishing of horsetails	manna sweet	heart-clenching	savoury
paradise-green	the trembling of leaves	march pane sweet	heart-clamping	scrumptious
Shangri-La green	the whinnying of foals	marzipan sweet	heart-pumping	sumptuous
utopian-green	the whirring of dragonflies	meringue sweet	heart-thumping	tantalising
Valhalla-green	the whittling of gardeners	nougat sweet	skin-tingling	toothsome
Zion-green	the yelping of fox cubs	treacle sweet	jaw-dropping	wholesome

SUMMER

SEA-BLUE RIVERS	SOFT SOUNDS	LOUD SOUNDS	COSMIC SMELLS	MOVEMENT OF SMELLS
aquarium-blue	the chittering of swallows	clip-clopping horses	astral	blew
Atlantic-blue	the chugging of rivers	chattering starlings	astronomical	carried
Atlantis-blue	the cooing of pigeons	champing cows	cosmic	drafted
Baltic-blue	the crooning of songbirds	cropping sheep	galactic	drifted
Caribbean-blue	the drenching of showers	glopping raindrops	otherworldly	floated
Mediterranean-blue	the drifting of clouds	gurgling rivers	out-of-this-world	glided
Neptune-blue	the fluting of blackbirds	masticating cows	out-of-this-universe	ghosted
Pacific-blue	the huffing of the breeze	munching sheep	stellar	rushed
Sargasso-blue	the hush of the land	neighing horses	transcendental	sailed
riparian-blue	the lingering moon	nickering foals	unearthly	strayed

SUMMER

SKY BLUES	SOFT SOUNDS	LOUD SOUNDS	A MIX OF SMELLS	VERBS FOR SMELLS
aurora-blue skies	the lisping of rills	plunking fish	a barbecue of smells	languished in
birthstone-blue skies	the lolling of lake boats	pumping heart of summer	a brew of smells	leisured in
chemical-blue skies	the lowing of cows	quivering wheat fields	a broth of smells	lingered in
cocktail-blue skies	the mumbling of bees	scrunching leaves	a buffet of smells	loitered in
constellation-blue skies	a murmuring of the wind	sizzling summers	a burgoo of smells	lounged in
electric-blue skies	murmurations of water	sloshing fish	a chowder of smells	passed through
halogen-blue skies	the nuzzling of foals	sploshing salmon	a goulash of smells	percolated through
halcyon-blue skies	the piping of blackbirds	spluttering streams	a menu of smells	phantomed through
lodestar-blue skies	the purling of rivulets	sputtering rain	a stew of smells	pilfered through
polaris-blue skies	the purring of runnels	tintinnabulation of water	a soup of smells	puffed through

SUMMER

BLUE WATERFALLS	SOFT SOUNDS	LOUD SOUNDS	A MIX OF SMELLS	WORDS FOR SMELLS
cerulean-blue	the skimming of swallows	warbling songbirds	a carnival of smells	the aroma of
plasma-blue	the soughing of the wind	whittling gardeners	a carousel of smells	the bouquet of
silk-blue	the sprinkling of hoses	whirruping waterfalls	a cornucopia of smells	the cologne of
satin-blue	the swirling of wheat fields	whizzing falling stars	a circus of smells	the fragrance of
star blaze-blue	the trickling of rills	whooshing comets	a funfair of smells	the olfactory overload of
star flame-blue	the throbbing heart of	wobbling ice creams	a pageant of smells	perfume of
solar-blue	thrumming hooves of foals	yipping foxes	a riot of smells	the redolence of
suede-blue	the trilling of thrushes	zinging waterfalls	a smorgasbord of smells	the scent of
velvet-blue	the tweeting of chicks	zipping hawks	a tapestry of smells	the waft of
velour-blue	the whisking of wheat ears	zooming falcons	a theatre of smells	the whiff of

AUTUMN

AUTUMN REDS	AUTUMN GOLDS	SOFT SOUNDS	LOUD SOUNDS	DECIDUOUS SMELLS
barbecue-reds	gleaming-golds	the caressing of the wind	battering winds	clay-rich
bonfire-reds	glinting-golds	the chirruping of songbirds	blasting storms	earthy
conflagration-reds	glittering-golds	the crinkling of leaves	boiling skies	loamy
crematorium-reds	glowing-golds	the crisping of flaky leaves	booming thunder	mushroomy
ember-reds	lightning-golds	the crumbling of vegetation	buffeting squalls	mulchy
incinerator-reds	luminous-golds	the droning of the dragonflies	caterwauling windstorms	oaken
inferno-reds	lustrous-golds	the hooting of owls	cawing ravens	organic
lava-reds	molten-golds	the lapping of water	churning clouds	peaty
magma-reds	sunburst-golds	the lilting tones of autumn	clawing warlocks	seasoned
pyre-reds	waxmelt-golds	the muffled forest sounds	creeping crawlies	woody

AUTUMN

AUTUMN REDS	AUTUMN ORANGES	SOFT SOUNDS	LOUD SOUNDS	CONIFEROUS SMELLS
claret-reds	fiery-oranges	the phut-phut of falling nuts	crunching cannibals	the amber whiff of
haemoglobin-reds	flaming-oranges	the pulsing soul of autumn	drooling ogres	the glycerine aroma of
oxblood-reds	blazing-oranges	the puling of the soft winds	echoing sounds	the gummy fragrance of
marrow-reds	broiling-oranges	the quavering of wrens' wings	exploding toadstools	the medicinal scent of
rushlight-reds	burning-oranges	the rustling of leaves	guzzling gorgons	the minty tint of
Titian-reds	incandescent-oranges	the shuddering of trees	heaving seas	the pine sweet cologne of
vermeil-reds	scorching-oranges	the shuffling of forest walkers	howling wolves	the resin sweet pot pourri of
vermilion-reds	smouldering-oranges	the silence of the dawn	keening north winds	the sap sweet redolence of
vinaceous-reds	sweltering-oranges	the snuffling of whiskey-noses	prowling ghosts	the starch sweet hotchpotch of
windfall-reds	volcanic-oranges	the squelching of feet	raging rivers	the thyme sweet perfume of

AUTUMN

AUTUMN REDS	AUTUMN YELLOWS	SOFT SOUNDS	LOUD SOUNDS	FRUITY SMELLS
balefire-reds	brimstone-yellows	the slumbering of hedgehogs	scrawling goblins	citrus sharp
brazier-reds	candle flame-yellows	the tinkling of waterfalls	skittering animals	fruitcake heavy
devil blood-reds	feverish-yellows	the twirling of leaves	sissing rain	full bodied
dragon flame-reds	flashing-yellows	the twittering of songbirds	slobbering trolls	mead sweet
firebrand-reds	flickering-yellows	the wheezing of the wind	slurping vampires	melon ripe
firedrake-reds	hot-yellows	the whirling of leaves	splintering boughs	orchard sweet
firefly-reds	incendiary-yellows	the whimpering of the wind	suppurating floods	peachy
glow worm-reds	moon flame-yellows	the whispering of wheat fields	wailing witches	pear ripe
hellhound-reds	sulphur-yellows	the yawning of the wind	yowling banshees	plummy
phoenix-reds	sultry-yellows	the yawl of fog horns	zinging raindrops	windfall sweet

CALM SEA SOUNDS

A dreamy sea has a rhythmic pulse to it unmatched by any other part of nature. It forges its own sounds and kindles its own symphony. The following 50 sentences are an attempt to capture the song of the sea and its steady, throbbing heartbeat. If you find yourself visualising its glorious vastness, its dreamy surface and straining to hear its metronomic wave music, you may understand why it's called the fisherman's friend.

1. The sea was **buzzing** with its dormant strength.
2. The waves were **crawling** gently to the shore.
3. The waves were **creeping** steadily towards us.
4. The **dreamy** sea was its own master.
5. The waves were gently **drenching** the sand.
6. The sea softly **doused** the beach.
7. The waves were carelessly **dribbling** onto the sand.
8. The **ebbing** tide was harmonious.
9. The sea was vaporously **exhaling** its mist.
10. The **flowing** of the tide was languorous.
11. The ocean was **forging** its own sea-song.
12. The **gasping** waves were waiting for full tide.
13. The **groaning** sea was riparian-blue.
14. The **gurgling** waves were metronomic.
15. The **gushing** waves were comforting.
16. The **humming** of the wave-song beguiled me.
17. The sea was **kindling** its own symphony.
18. The **lapping** waves entranced us.
19. The **murmuring** of the waves was hypnotic.
20. The waves were **oozing** onto the beach.
21. The **palpitating** pulse of the sea was steady and peaceful.
22. The **plinking** of the wave-music was enthralling.
23. The **pulsing** sea was acetylene-blue.
24. The **quivering** sea was hoarding its mighty power.
25. The **quavering** sea harnessed its majesty.

CALM SEA SOUNDS

26. The waves were **rippling** the feather soft sand.
27. The sea spray was **showering** the beach.
28. The **sighing** of the waves was mesmerising.
29. The **simpering** waves had a seductive-blue hue.
30. The **shuddering** waves held back their latent power.
31. The **sleepy** sea was entangled in its own dreams.
32. The **slothful** sea was supine.
33. The sea was moving like a **sluggard** in sleep walk.
34. The **slumbering** sea was best left alone.
35. The **snoozy** sea heaved gently.
36. The **spiralling** sea was rolling with its own majesty.
37. The **splashing** waves were waiting for full tide.
38. The **sprinkling** spray was wraith-white.
39. The **spluttering** waves sounded like a gulping burp.
40. The **swelling** sea suddenly stilled.
41. The sea was **swirling** the seashells.
42. The **symphonious** sea was creating a wave murmur.
43. The **throbbing** sea was leavening like slow-rising dough.
44. The **tintinnabulation** of the sea was musical.
45. The **trembling** sea was plasma-blue.
46. The sea was **twirling** the flotsam around.
47. The **whirling** sea created the wave hum.
48. The **whirring** of the waves was as soft as a lullaby.
49. The **whimpering** of the sea foretold the storm.
50. The mighty **yawning** of the sea didn't fool us. We knew a Reckoning was coming…..

ANGRY SEA SOUNDS

Just like a snoozy sea can be the fisherman's friend, a violent sea can be his nautical nemesis. It can simmer in its malice and be raspy and dissonant in its rage. The following 50 sentences attempt to capture the wild majesty of an angry sea.

1. The waves were **bashing** the sullen cliffs.
2. The sea was **battering** the rocky shore.
3. The waves were **beating** against the craggy cliffs.
4. The sea was **belting** the glowering cliffs.
5. The waves were **bludgeoning** the pebble-dashed shore.
6. The sea was **bombarding** the shocked cliffs.
7. The feral sea was **booming** its displeasure.
8. The sea was **bubbling** and hissing.
9. The feckless sea was **buffeting** the cliffs.
10. The **cacophonous** sea was seething with spite.
11. The squally sea was **chafing** at the cliffs.
12. The **clangourous** sea unleashed its savagery.
13. The choppy waves were **clapping** like thunder.
14. The savage sea was **clattering** the shoreline.
15. The stormy waves were **clobbering** the cliffs.
16. The foaming sea was **clubbing** the shore.
17. The cavernous waves were **crushing** the little seashells.
18. The frothy sea was **gnawing** at the cliffs.
19. The lathering sea was **growling** in anger.
20. The ferocious waves were **howling** towards the shore.
21. The boiling sea was **hurtling** the wave tops in its rage.
22. The fierce sea was **lacerating** the cliffs.
23. The maniacal sea was **lathering** itself into frenzy.
24. The wind-tossed sea was **lashing** the cliffs.
25. The wicked waves were **pummelling** the shoreline.

ANGRY SEA SOUNDS

26. The **plunging** sea was brutal in its intensity.
27. The **pounding** sea was buckling the waves.
28. The **roaring** waves were froth-fuelled.
29. The **screaming** of the sea was like a banshee's wail.
30. The waves were **slapping** furiously at the cliffs.
31. The **slobbering** sea licked hungrily at the cliffs.
32. The **slashing** waves of the tsunami were monstrous.
33. The **slopping** sea chewed angrily at the cliffs.
34. The **sloshing** waves wore away the august cliffs.
35. The **slurping** of the sea was relentless.
36. The **smacking** waves were remorseless.
37. The **smashing** waves were cannibalising the cliffs.
38. The **snarling** waves were froth-white with rage.
39. The sea was **spitting** with its own splenetic anger.
40. The sea was **splashing** in its own bilious rage.
41. The **splattering** waves carved age-old carnage into the cliffs.
42. The sea was **spewing** out its timeless spite.
43. The sea was **stewing** in its bruised-blue hatred.
44. The seething sea was **surging** towards the shore.
45. The vengeful sea was **suppurating** the cliffs.
46. The waves were **walloping** the startled cliffs.
47. The maniacal sea was **whipping** itself into insanity.
48. The tsunami's giant waves were **whooshing** towards land.
49. The **writhing** sea was demonic in its intensity.
50. The **zesty** sea had spent itself. It was over.

FORMULAS FOR A HORIZON AND A SEA SKY

HORIZON

VASTNESS	SHAPE	COLOUR	KNITTING TERMS
The boundless	arc of	astral-blue was	braided with silver.
The endless	arch of	brochure-blue was	edged with silver.
The indefinite	crescent of	celestial-blue was	fringed with silver clouds.
The infinite	dome of	constellation-blue was	hemmed with silver.
The limitless	vault of	halogen-blue was	knitted with silver.

SKY

VASTNESS	FABRICS	COLOUR	KNITTING TERMS
The measureless	blanket of	neon-blue was	laced with angel-white clouds.
The never ending	cloak of	paradise-blue was	seamed with cloud-tufts.
The unfathomable	drape of	plasma-blue was	sewn with puffball-white.
The unending	mantle of	solar-blue was	stitched with tuft-clouds.
The unlimited	veil of	stratosphere-blue was	threaded with flimsy clouds.

THE MOVEMENT OF BIRDS IN THE AIR

SWALLOWS	SEAGULLS	STORM PETRELS	EAGLES
arrowing through	lazing in	gyrating in	arcing in
darting through	loitering in	pirouetting in	banking in
flinging through	languishing in	reeling in	circling in
flitting through	lolling in	spinning in	floating in
slinging through	lounging in	twirling in	gliding in
whirling through	looping in	wheeling in	hovering in

By using the motion of birds in the air, you are providing imagery that is non-linear. That was discussed on page 3. It is always good to keep varying the angles of narration for the reader. In this way, the reader keeps more of an interest in the story as it is multi-faceted. The golden rule of descriptive writing is; look up, look down and then look around. When that level of excellence has been reached, you may find yourself looking **into** the soul of a scene.

100 MAGICAL WORDS FOR AN ESSAY

velvet	lush	carnival	mellifluous	exquisite
mystique	phosphorescence	angel fire	opulence	pixie dust
ravishing	glimmering	luxurious	jasper	toothsome
lemongrass	sleek	ethereal	lucerne	sizzling
bliss	sorcery	svelte	hallucinatory	incarnadine
tantalising	rill	owl light	assuages	dulcet
languorous	arcipluvian	misty-eyed	lissome	sensuous
alchemy	lithe	twirling	sorbet	juicy
vermilion	ephemeral	sumptuous	plush	elysian
tinkling	salubrious	paradise	shimmering	stellar
supple	murmurs	wood sorrel	gloaming	dewy-eyed
halcyon	phantasm-grey	flourishing	iridescent	sparkling
frazil	placid	star flash	cloudberry	glassy
evanescent	rapture	aurora	oxblood	alluring
luminous	crystalline	soughing	glamour	cerise
fragrance	transcendental	beryl	swirling	magnetism
serene	lucid	mystical	cinnamon	eunoia
voluptuous	starless	claret-red	thaumaturgy	river gazer
honey dew	fuchsia-pink	whirring	opaline	Amazonian
Arcadian	elf light	splendour	monk hum	stardust

These words are some of the most beautiful and resonant in the English language. Each one should have the effect of improving a passage of writing. A lot of them are **phonoaesthetic,** which means they have a quality of sound that appeals to people. That is why Tolkien, Edgar Allen Poe, Japanese, Italians and Spanish people amongst others all love the word: **CELLAR DOOR.** The fact that it is two words didn't seem to concern them! My own personal favourite is frazil-silver. Frazil is the archaic term for the ice crystals tumbling down a mountain stream. If there's a better image out there than shiny, frazil-silver ice crystals cascading down a birthstone-blue mountain stream, I would love to hear about it!

100 OTHER MAGICAL WORDS AND COLOURS

pulsar	beguiling	pristine	fluting	soul-swelling
nectarine	thrumming	earthlight-gold	spellbinding	windfall-red
emollient	hallowed	vivacious	rush light-red	lapping
gossamer	cambering	enchanting	divine	melange
translucence	illusory	otherworldly	paradise-green	warbling
ultramarine	rhapsody	burbling	jewel dust	a-smoulder
infinity	argent-silver	chartreuse	earthshine-gold	lavish
lambent	manna	saccharine	cascaded	petrichor
celestial	sublime	euphonious	lilting	enthralling
fairytale-green	willowy	halogen-blue	emblazoned	hosanna
a-flash	bucolic	velour	sylvan	moonbeams
quivering	orpine-purple	wizard-white	Titian-red	a-light
glamour dust	trilling	minty	mystique	eldritch
geosmine	honeysuckle	riparian	sprinkling	luminol-blue
larimar-blue	dawn-pink	nut-brown	empyrean	confectionary
chiming	effervescent	luminous	shimmering	salve
pellucid	sylph-like	glistering	heavenly	oxblood-red
magenta	lolling	succulent	purling	unearthly
luscious	vaporous	languid	vista	potpourri
argent-silver	polestar-blue	Tyrian-purple	saffron-orange	Eden-green

A great exercise to test someone's English skills is to divide the words into rows of 5 or columns of twenty. Using a dictionary if necessary, try to compose a story using those words. Repeat the exercise regularly and you will find that your English skills will be much improved. Not only does it broaden your diction, but it also helps you to manipulate words into their proper context. If you can think of more beautiful words, you should keep them in a special section in your vocabulary notebook. The word 'eunoia' means 'beautiful thinking'. My hope is that by reading this book, all those who like to progress at English will write with both eunoia and stardust. Thanks, God bless, and may you prosper.

Author's Bio

Liam O' Flynn has been an English teacher in St. Aidan's Community College in Cork for the past twenty years. In that time, he has taught to a whole range of abilities and ages with considerable success. He is 43 years of age and single but in a long term relationship. A resident of Clonmel, he is a dedicated member of the writers' group there.

Liam's interests are: descriptive writing, nature walks, golf and fishing. He keeps a log of the birds who visit his garden, as one does, and has reached the grand total of 32 species. To the peregrine falcon and the sparrow hawk, species number 31 and 32, he has only two words: go away. His next book shall be an adventure/fantasy book for teenagers.

Thanks to Attracta, Brigid, Dave, Mary, Michael, Paddy and Tony from the writers' group. Each of you is talented, gracious and special and I treasure the Tuesday nights with you all.

Thanks to Frank Costigan, Tony and Adrian. You know why.

Special thanks also to Bernard, Danielle and Pat, lifeboats on a stormy sea.

Thanks to Davey K; a friend in need is a friend indeed.

To my wonderful girlfriend Lillian, my brothers Alan, Derek and Ray, my sister Gemma, my father Liam and mother Phil and my great friends Fergal, Rossi and Paul; cheers for the support everyone. You are always in my thoughts.

Printed in Great Britain
by Amazon.co.uk, Ltd.,
Marston Gate.